4

D0924416

Rural America, an Old Man, and a Harley

a Memoir

DAVID RICKERSON Sr.

ISBN-13: 9798766996002

Contents

Prologue

The open road has called out to travelers since long before the invention of the automobile —the romantic notions of freedom, the echoes of hobos riding the rails, wagon trains filled with families crossing the prairies, young people hitchhiking across America during the 60s and 70s looking for answers, or soul mates running away from home.

Most folks have a yearning to experience the open road. As if it were an entity unto itself, it calls us from distant lands with the promise of a brighter tomorrow.

Over the last century, hundreds of songs have been written, the anthem of the highways and byways. The Eagles, The Beatles, Roger Miller, Johnny Cash, and many other artists have written and played tunes that whet our appetites for travel and adventure.

The song that most likely inspired my journey was from a little-known singer/songwriter, Rosie Thomas, her 2002 song "Wedding Day." It's a story about a girl who was "wronged" in love. She's packed her car and is looking forward to life as she drives aimlessly, searching for a new beginning. Whatever the case may be, I somehow feel the reasons to leave the comfort and safety of our homes may be connected. I hope to provide a glimpse of that connection here.

In this book, you'll experience, through my eyes, a way to travel that I believe we're losing touch with. I hope you'll find something here to ignite a fire deep inside to make the changes you fear.

Someone wiser than I once said, "Pain isn't in the change, but in the resistance to change."

The reason we resist change is generally because of the fear of the unknown. As I traveled, I found people to be warm and genuine. However, there was one particular night that wasn't the case. I felt unsafe and threatened. But I continued on my journey as I battled the elements on dark country roads that wound through hills with little or no shoulders. The occasional oncoming car blinded me. My glasses were fogged and spotted from the rain and mist, and my destination was still almost two hours away, leaving me to wonder how I would summon the courage to forge ahead.

The Decision

My wife Katie and I had organized a vacation to the Jersey Shore with another couple, Nichole and Tom, for almost nine months. Tom and I had planned on driving his truck to Jersey. First, we would go to Daytona Beach, then head north on A1A, through Jacksonville, and along the coast, taking the ferries to Ocracoke and Hatteras, the Outer Banks in North Carolina, up Rt.12, then across the Bay Bridge Tunnel into Maryland. Finally, we would head up through Delaware into Southern New Jersey, where he and I grew up. At the same time, our wives would fly to NYC and stay in Times Square for a few days. They would rent a car there in early September, then meet us in Wildwood, NJ.

My marriage had been in trouble for some time. Arguments regularly became overwhelming. I don't believe either of us was very happy, and I asked for a divorce in May. My wife obliged by drafting the divorce papers. She then suggested we take six months, saying, "You work on you, I'll work on me."

I thought that to be a splendid idea and agreed. I put the divorce papers in the safe.

This was my third marriage, and I was not getting much better at it. However, I felt Katie, and I were willing to try. But just two days later, she insisted I decide whether we'd stay together.

I'm not the kind of guy who could be strong-armed into a decision. I never cared much for ultimatums either. I replied, "Then let's divorce."

I thought the planned vacation might do us good, but Katie wouldn't hear of it. So I talked with Tom about the three of us going anyway, but it wouldn't be the same without Katie.

Tom was a motorcycle enthusiast. He owned a Harley Davidson Road King. I had always wanted a Harley but wouldn't part with the money. Anyway, riding a motorcycle in Florida is an insane idea. We have tourists who drive on the wrong side of the road and oodles of overmedicated seniors who shouldn't be driving unless they're on a kiddie ride at Chuck E Cheese. Then we have kids chewing gum and texting while they steer with their knees and the occasional carjacker running from the law, blowing lights, and driving into oncoming traffic at Mach 1 speeds.

I'd been hit head-on twice since 1997, once in an E-250 Ford van and once in a Ford Ranger, totaling both of my vehicles. Both times I was in my lane doing the speed limit. I applied evasive maneuvers to no avail. The on-comers chased me down for the kill. Both drivers were in their mid-90s. So a long time ago, I decided never to own a motorcycle while I lived in Florida. That is, until November of last year.

My son Ty got married and failed to invite anyone from his side of the family. He didn't ask his sister, mother, or grandmother, who had put a roof over his head for some time. Or myself. I was fairly upset with him when I found out.

I called Tallahassee the next morning and requested a refund of his prepaid college fund. I figured if he wanted to go to college, he could pay for it himself. He might appreciate it more if he had to work for it. When the check came, I paid off a couple of debts and considered buying a Harley.

I had two sisters. Julie died in a nursing home at sixty-two, and my oldest sister, Lori, is in a nursing home now. I hadn't been able to see her since before COVID started. I thought, *If I die on a motorcycle, I'm a step ahead of either of them.*

So I began to obsess over finding the perfect bike at a great price.

It took just a few weeks. I bought a used Harley Softail Slim with 4,170 miles on it. The price was more than reasonable. The bike was garaged in Cocoa Beach, about three hours from my home. I have an '05 Scion XB with a trailer hitch, so I rented a motorcycle trailer from U-Haul and headed out.

The bike belonged to a woman in her late forties. Her husband started the bike and rode it around the lot, curling into the throttle a little. It sounded so good with the Vance and Hines pipes. He offered me the chance to ride it, but I declined. I was afraid of it.

I paid for her, and we put it on the trailer and cinched it down well. I drove home, so proud, at eighty mph with that small car and my first Harley.

I already had the endorsement on my license, but two of my friends, Tom and Tim, convinced me to take the motorcycle safety course. Both were experienced riders, and I respected their judgment. Also, they had ridden for many years and still had taken the course.

In my younger years, I owned four motorcycles. I knew how to ride, but I took the class anyway with an open mind. Tom gave me a gift certificate that paid for over half of the fees.

The course, offered at Bert's Barracuda Harley Davidson in Pinellas Park, was a three-day course. One in the classroom, two on the course. It was extensive, even for beginners. The plus was that I trained on their motorcycle. If I had crashed or dropped the bike, it wasn't mine.

I learned much more than I ever thought I would. Since I was fifteen, I have been riding motorcycles, but this really made me aware of my surroundings and has probably saved me loads of money and heartache. One dropped motorcycle can cost several hundred dollars or more, let alone getting whacked. I believe all motorists should take this course. It would surely make the roadways safer.

When my class completed the course, we were given our diplomas and then ushered into the showroom.

A voice came over the intercom requesting everyone's attention. The speaker welcomed the new class of inductees into the Harley Davidson family. Every employee of this facility stood at attention next to a bike. The bikes were simultaneously started and revved up inside the huge showroom. The roar shook my very soul. I was utterly overwhelmed. It's an experience I'll never forget.

The longest trip I had ever taken on a motorcycle was two months later in March to Daytona with Tom. We took the scenic route as opposed to the highways. Florida in the spring produces some amazing weather for riding a motorcycle. If it's planned properly, you can travel through the orange groves when the blossoms have the sweetest aroma; it's intoxicating.

The three-and-a-half-hour ride turned into an over five-hour exercise in survival. I soon found it difficult to understand how guys could ride 1000 miles on one of these sleds in a couple of days. My ass was sore. I had cramps in my hands and wrists, and the wind at 70mph beat me to death.

I was sixty-five years old, with various ailments, although I still got around pretty well. I thought a long ride on a motorcycle was out of the question.

Louis, another local friend locally, had taken some long road trips to Sturgis, South Dakota, and Laconia bike week. I was baffled how he could make it there in two or three days.

I had been trying to figure a way to trailer the bikes north and then just ride back down through the mountains. Taking our time, Shenandoah is beautiful, the Smokies, the Appalachian Mountains, and the Asheville area, maybe from Pennsylvania south.

Tom and I discussed possibly driving to New York to visit Bethel Woods (Woodstock). I had taken my teenage daughter there a couple of years ago for the fiftieth anniversary. I wanted to return there, but the chances of taking that journey were gone now, with the entire trip canceled. At least I got my deposit back from the house we intended to rent.

Then I started to think...

Since I had tucked away some money for this trip, why couldn't I ride my bike North?

"Nah, that's crazy!"

I knew Tom wouldn't go. I would have to go alone. As crazy as that sounded, I began to formulate a plan.

I needed to buy a windshield. I found one on Marketplace for $200.00. It was new in the box. I had to drive an hour to pick it up, but it included docking hardware which allowed the windshield to be removed quickly. I would need to be able to carry luggage, but saddlebags on an FLS, without lots of modifications, would be small. I found a set, but I realized I needed brackets once I got them home. A sissy bar would be required to carry a T-bag.

I began planning my route and searching to find everything else I needed, either used or discounted, because I was recently retired and working on a shoestring budget. I even picked up a throttle assist in helping with cramping, and I also purchased a small tent.

In planning the route and stops, I downloaded an app to find free or cheap camping sites nationwide, and apps for navigation and packed a backup GPS. I also bought wiring for a power source.

I packed the bike several times to see how it would work. Was it stable? I tried packing different clothes. Should I take my leather coat? It was summer… I went over and over things in my head.

Even after I got it all figured out, the bike sat parked in the garage for several days while I awaited a window of good weather. I would be gone for three weeks, maybe.

I wanted to travel 200 - 250 miles a day. I thought I would begin my trip by riding to Macon, Georgia, to see the Allman Brothers Museum (The Big House) and Rose Hill Cemetery, where Duane and Greg are buried, with Butch Trucks and Barry Oakley.

I had been there once before. Katie planned a vacation for us several years ago.

From Macon, I would drive North to see friends in Asheville. Then I would work my way up through the Carolinas to Virginia, then Pennsylvania, where I had family I hadn't seen in several years. My cousin John lives in a house that's been in my family for almost 100 years.

I hoped to head East to New York to see close friends, south to Woodstock, and then to New Jersey to see my remaining sister and family.

I didn't think I would be able to get there, but I dreamed. If anything, I thought I might make it to Asheville, then come home with my tail between my legs.

The weather wasn't cooperative, and at home, I sat. I had rain gear, but something was missing: gumption. Deep down inside, I was terrified to leave. I'd never attempted anything like this. Yeah, I'd taken road trips in rental cars, but I'd call the rental company to bring me another vehicle if the rental car broke down. I'd also taken trips in my vehicle, too. Usually, I had someone along with me. But going alone on a bike was more than a little scary.

I figured I had a pretty good shot at not having too many issues with the bike. It only had about 7,000 miles on it when I left. But even so, there were some real fears. I wasn't that experienced, especially riding in the rain or on hills. What if I had a wreck? What if I failed? What if

I lost confidence? What if I got sick? What if I got robbed? I considered getting a concealed carry permit.

Saturday, June 19th, tropical storm Claudette made landfall in Louisiana. It was headed close to where I had planned to stop the first night. There was another storm brewing at home. I could stay no longer. My wife asked me to leave and stay away, so I left.

I got on the bike with a myriad of emotions: fear, despair, anger, and hopelessness. I felt like a kid running away from home with nowhere to go. Instead of taking the back roads, I jumped on I-275 and headed North to I-75.

Although I had left later than I wanted, I felt I needed to put some miles behind me. I did what I didn't want to do. I got in a hurry. When I reached Ocala, traffic was stopped. Sitting in traffic in a car is difficult; it's absolutely no fun on a motorcycle.

It was a hot summer day. The heat from the bike's motor was rising around my legs. I thought I smelled hot dogs cooking; it was my thighs. Sweat poured off me, and as if the exhaust fumes weren't bad enough, someone was smoking pot. It was all I could smell, and the thought of someone being stoned while I was operating a motorcycle was scary. I thought, *Well, maybe that's why they call it the highway.*

Eventually, traffic started moving, and I got onto US-301, to I-10, to I-95 north. By the time I got to Georgia, my ass hurt, and I had cramps in my hands. I needed some rest, and motels were expensive on a Saturday evening around Savannah. This was one of the reasons I wanted to leave early in the week.

I found a spot, but it wasn't cheap.

From the hotel, I phoned Marsha, an old friend. I figured she'd be awake, and she was. Marsha worked as a nurse on the overnight shift. She and her husband, Rob, moved to Asheville some years ago.

"Marsha! What are you doing? I'm in Savannah. I'm coming for a visit."

"Oh shit, Rickerson. I'm not home. I'm in Florida with my sister. Rob is in Fayetteville. We bought a house there," she replied.

"Well, I was hoping to see you and have you show me around Asheville."

"Y'know what? My neighbor Deb has the key. I'll send you the address. Get the key and stay as long as you like. I'll call Deb."

I had my next destination. That was all I needed, was someplace to point my nose.

Heading North

Sunday Morning was beautiful! I decided right then to stay off highways. I got coffee, and soon enough, I was back on the Harley, becoming excited about this trip.

About an hour into the ride, the sky began to darken. Suddenly the rain started to fall. I looked for a place to hide out. There were not many overpasses on the back roads. I was on a stretch of Route 23, where gas stations weren't plentiful either. I got wet. I finally found a parking lot to pull into. It was a toy shop called "Playthings Etc. Family Toy & Hobbies." It looked like some kind of a spaceship.

I stopped and removed my rain gear from the pack behind me. I had yet to try it on, mistake #1. In the parking lot was a heavy-set older man, tipping over, trying to get his trousers on. Not only did the britches have Velcro, but they also zipped up on the outside of the legs. Unzipping was the easy part. The hard part was keeping the Velcro from closing as I danced around with one foot in the air, attempting to push my boot through the already closed pant leg.

To make matters worse, I had neuropathy in both feet. My balance wasn't the best.

After several unsuccessful tries, I was out of breath and soaking wet. Finally, both legs were in, and the pants buttoned.

The jacket was somewhat easier.

I didn't think the store was open just yet, so anyone who may have witnessed the "dancing lard-ass" was passersby. I thought for sure there would be a video on YouTube by now.

I got back on my bike and took off. The rain continued off and on. The sky began to clear an hour or so down the road. I turned around on "Old U.S. 25," where I had spotted a road that looked interesting, "Callahan Mountain Rd." I turned onto that and rode just a short while, looking for something scenic and a place to rest.

Along the north side were beautiful tall pine trees. The scent seemed to call to me. I pulled onto the shoulder and put the kickstand down. I thought the most comfortable spot would be with the front wheel cocked to the left. I could sit on the ground, lean against the bike, and doze off.

That's one of the things about me. I can sleep anywhere and can get there relatively quickly.

I probably only dozed for ten to twenty minutes, but that was enough to refresh me. After a few minutes,

I got on the bike and headed back to Rt. 25. I was still an hour away from Asheville.

At some point, I stopped and looked at my maps and realized I was very close to North Saluda Reservoir. I thought that would be a great place to explore, but the weather looked "iffy," so maybe next time. Continuing on, I arrived in Asheville just before dark.

This was the first time my Harley would be left out in the rain. I had purchased ceramic coating for the bike from "Car Candy" before I left for the trip. I did extensive research on available ceramic coatings. Their huge product line had great reviews and was reasonably priced. The best part when I called was that I was connected to a human being immediately. Geri hand-delivered my kit. She gave me detailed instructions on how to apply it.

My son David details cars. He buffed out two minor scratches and all the swirl marks. He then used a clay bar to clean any impurities from the surface. We wiped everything down with the cleaner provided by "Car Candy" to remove all oils from fingerprints and such.

Dave took his time and put on liberal coats of the "Car Candy" ceramic coating, especially focusing on the front forks. They get most of the abuse from road dirt, bugs & pebbles.

Today, they still look new. We even did the Vance & Hines pipes. The ceramic coating withstands high temperatures.

When I arrived at Marsha's place, Deb helped me get squared away. She made us a coffee at her place, and we chatted for some time like we had been friends for years.

The next couple of days would find me riding around Asheville, getting accustomed to riding, stopping, and turning on hills.

As I checked out the scenery, I found an old brick building downtown with what looked to be an ancient Coca-Cola advertisement painted on the wall. I'm an amateur photographer and am always looking for photo opportunities. This was it.

I turned and pulled into the parking lot. There just happened to be an opening to place the bike, perfect for the shot that I wanted. There were two Coca-Cola advertisements on the same wall. One painted on top of the other. With the Bobber-style motorcycle in the foreground, it seemed a perfect shot.

I rode along the French Broad River through Marshall. I stopped at places to look at the river and take pictures. I found a small park and stopped to walk around to take in the beauty.

It was so easy just to continue to drive by and miss the majesty of God's handiwork. This trip was about doing something different.

As I traveled outside the Asheville area, I found an old, abandoned gas station/repair shop. The garage doors were long gone, and the building had no windows. Here was another photo opportunity. I pulled in and took several shots of my Harley from different angles with the beautiful vintage backdrop.

Later that day, as I returned to Asheville, I was somewhat taken aback to find the homeless situation around the town to be what it was. Folks camped alongside roadways with clothes and what appeared to be trash strewn about.

I have no problem with folks being homeless by choice. Many people want that lifestyle, but it comes with little responsibility. I've known many people who camped out for long periods. What I don't get is why people would leave trash everywhere. I was taught to leave it better than I found it.

Deb was kind enough to take me around Asheville to sightsee and grab dinner on my last night there. We stopped in several shops, but my ability to transport souvenirs home was nil, so I bought candy instead. I'll always find a spot for that.

The next morning, I tidied up Marsha and Rob's place, put the trash out, and packed up the bike. I rode north toward Scottsville, Va. I didn't have a route picked and had planned on stopping midway.

I had downloaded an app that showed campgrounds, many of which were free, but I didn't find the app user-friendly, so I figured I'd just wing it. I'd always wanted to take a trip where I could wake up, pick some grass, throw it up in the air, and whichever way the grass blew, follow that lead until I found something interesting and stopped for as long as I wanted. There I was, on the back roads that twisted through the hills of North Carolina, doing just that.

The landscape in North Carolina was stunning and peaceful along the Blue Ridge Parkway, and the overlooks were plentiful. I stopped at various places to take photos. It was a bit of a struggle for me to do so at first. I'd trained myself to travel in straight lines. The superhighways had little tolerance for wanderers who wished to photograph or enjoy. I had to force myself to pull off, to explore.

On and off the Blue Ridge Parkway, I rode throughout the day. I found that being off the parkway was the most interesting; the old barns and vacant old wooden homes that were falling down. Such beautiful parts of Americana were easily seen and photographed there.

It was almost 6 pm when I stumbled upon "Raccoon Holler Campground" in Jefferson, NC. The office was just about to close. The women were ready to leave when I pulled in.

The fee was reasonable enough. I was handed a map and told to drive down the rise, turn left, and find the grassy area. The clerk said I would find another biker across the street from my site.

I rode through the campground and found my site. I saw the other bike parked across the way. I pulled into my spot and shut the bike down. As I did, I heard the fella say, "Hey, quit making all that racket over there," in this deep, raspy voice, with a thick Southern accent.

Across the street stood a fella over six feet, I'd say 275 pounds, beard, bald, and a biker vest, with all the patches. He approached me as he spoke.

Now I don't consider myself the biker type of guy. I guess maybe sometimes I'm intimidated by those that are. I don't dress the part, other than jeans and a leather jacket. I wear jeans because I'm not crazy about the idea of burning the flesh off my legs. Hot pipes are very unforgiving, and road rash isn't much fun. I wear a leather jacket because it can protect me, as well.

The man extended his hand and said, "My name is Robert, but my friends call me Peaches." And with a smile, he let out a big belly laugh.

Peaches stood next to the picnic table with one foot up on the bench and talked while I put my tent up for the first time. He told me he had owned many motorcycles over the years and how he had traveled to many states. He was a minister and a comedian (at least that day, he was). He was also a Vietnam Veteran. The stories of his life travels were quite amusing.

For most of my life, I've measured myself against other folks, and in my mind, I never seem quite to measure up. I knew I had to allow myself to be vulnerable and open up to him for some reason. That was a scary thought.

I explained to Peaches that this was my first voyage, and I had little experience. He assured me that I'd do just fine. I Was sure he could hear the uneasiness in my voice.

He was very kind, and we talked until long after dark. We shared funny stories. We laughed and laughed.

This would be my first-night camping with the bike. The tent had been rolled up in a sleeping bag, and both were covered with a trash bag. The T-Bag, a collapsible storage bag that mounts to the sissy bar, sat on the sleeping bag. Straps wrapped around the sleeping bag and the bike kept everything secure.

I pulled another trash bag over the waterproof T-Bag. I wrapped the entire package with a couple of twelve-foot black bungee cords. Everything had to come off the bike to get to the tent. Initially, I stored everything in the tent once it was set up. I discovered there wasn't room for the most important occupant...me. I couldn't stretch out (I'm only 5'-6"), and I soon realized I had to figure this stuff out.

The next morning, at first light, I heard Peaches just outside my tent, calling me to get up with that low, raspy voice. "C'mon, we're breaking camp and going for breakfast."

Now I was wrapped up in a military sleeping bag (cocoon) that was pretty warm, so I shivered when I got out of that thing. It was 53°. That was frostbite weather for me! You have to remember. I'm from Florida, where it's 85° at 6 am.

I rolled everything up, packed the bike, and thanked God I'd brought that leather jacket. I just wished I'd remembered to bring gloves.

We made a bit of racket rolling out of the campground and rode for about twenty minutes. The deer grazed along the way.

Peaches took the lead, and every time he saw something on the road, he'd point it out, so I was careful not to slip in leaves or gravel.

A doe stood pretty close to the road. I decided to scare her off the roadway, so I cracked my throttle twice, and she bolted off through the trees. As soon as I did that, I felt awful. I didn't like to mistreat animals. I'd tried to adopt some of the ideology from the Native American culture, where they treated all living beings like a little brother.

A friend once gave me a book to read, "Kinship With All Life." It changed much of how I viewed the world and how I was comfortable doing things. The funny thing was once I understood how the universe worked, I could no longer play dumb.

We pulled into the Shatley Springs Restaurant and Resort driveway, which would wind back along the lake and a fishing camp to the restaurant. It was a large red building with a big waiting area outside. I could tell this looked to be a bustling place at times. They were set up to handle a lot of traffic, but we were there early.

We were seated in the older part of the building, away from most other patrons. (I wondered why?) The tables had blue and white checkerboard tablecloths. This part of the structure looked to be at least 100 years old.

As the rather large waitress neared our table, it began to move. The floor seemed to have some structural issues. The salt and pepper shakers danced across the table. I stared at the tablecloth to keep from snickering while ordering coffee and food.

After eating, Peaches grabbed the check and wouldn't let me get the tip (maybe he thought I was Canadian). He said he would ride with me for an hour until he was ready to turn off to Salem, Winston.

The morning air was beginning to warm a little, and I felt more comfortable in the saddle. We pulled off to get a coffee and say goodbye. We exchanged phone numbers and rode off in our separate ways.

My next stop was to see Dan and Sharon in Scottsville, Va. I'd known them since about 1976. Dan and I took a small engine class together at the local vo-tech school in Mannington, NJ. He married Sharon when they were just sixteen, and they had three beautiful, successful daughters. In my eyes, they were the salt-of-the-earth kind of people.

Dan had purchased a photography business in Florida in about 1987. He was to get established first, then send for his family. When he called me with the news, I quickly made arrangements for him to stay with my mom in St. Petersburg.

Now my mom could be a funny woman. She was very caring, but she had her limits. Dan was only there a day or two when Mom began to circle ads in the local paper for housing and set them in front of Dan with his morning coffee. She was just about always that subtle.

I had called Dan to inform him of my visit to Virginia. He'd been asking me for years to see them. But his voice met me with, "We're in Florida."

I replied, "So... where's the key?"

They had neighbors watching their house and watering plants, and they expected to be home the day after my arrival. Dan texted me the address, and I continued toward his place.

I stopped at Civil War battlefields and historical places and overlooks along the way. I found one spot that had three old wagons along the road. A couple of historical markers told a story about the banjo and its origin. Many years ago, I had seen a black Banjo player, Otis Taylor. I'd never heard the blues played on a banjo before.

As he played for us in the intimate venue, he explained the banjo's history. I saw facts that reiterated what Otis had said, that "the Banjo was an African Instrument."

The rest of the ride that day was wonderful, with many detours.

I slowed down just a little more. I learned to relax my grip and enjoy the ride more with every mile.

I stayed with Dan and Sharon for three or four nights. The first night they weren't home. I had a spot in the garage for my bike next to Dan's bike. The first thing I did the following day was made myself a coffee.

I walked out to the back patio with a steaming mug in hand and sat in the morning light. The hummingbirds were already busy, along with bees, and the flowers they had were beautiful. Dan had said, "It's my "favorite-ist place on earth," and I could easily see why.

It just had peaceful energy about it. Dan was up early most mornings, watering the plants from his cisterns. He had a few varieties of tomatoes coming along nicely, and he had squash and more. All of the vegetables looked great.

Dan and Sharon weren't expected until late afternoon. I had some time to kill and wanted to explore this lovely countryside. I began to fall in love with Virginia.

The tiny town of Scottsville was on the James River, protected by a levy of sorts. One of the older buildings in town had hash marks and dates to identify each flood throughout the centuries.

I found Lumpkins restaurant, where I walked in, and it just smelled like home cooking. The service was good, and the food was great. I ate there a few more times.

I tried to attend an AA meeting in Charlottesville that evening. As I was nearing town, my phone screen began to act up, it turned green, and I couldn't see the map. I could hear the directions, but I was not going to try to find my way home without the GPS, so I turned around.

On the way, I pulled into a spot and reset the phone. It seemed OK, but I wondered if I had done something bad to the phone.

When Dan and Sharon returned from Florida that night, he inquired if I knew how to drive a zero-turn mower. I didn't and said so, but I was eager to try. It's a guy thing, I guess.

The next morning found me on the mower, right after coffee and breakfast. Dan suggested that I not run over the stumps, which he pointed out. I assured him I would not. Shortly after hitting the third stump, I decided to slow it down a little. I felt like I was in heaven.

The trees don't smell like much in Florida, nor does the grass when you mow it. But here, my olfactory senses were in paradise.

Some of the tree limbs were low. Dan and I later trimmed many of them and put them in his burn pile for the winter.

Sunday came, and I attended church for the first time in many years. It didn't cave in or even creak much. I had a good time. The sermon was simple, and the music was great! They did Facebook live on Sunday: "Bethlehem Life."

Dan had to work after the church services. He was a care provider for hospice. I cannot think of a kinder, gentler person for that job. I experienced his bedside manner once during a darker time in my life. That man saved my life. His loving kindness was unconditional and still is.

I spent a couple more days in Scottsville. I felt very much at home there. But I had to get on the road again.

On this leg of the journey, I had phoned ahead my cousin Tara and her husband, Eric. They lived in a suburb of Pittsburgh just north of the city. Leaving Scottsville, I traveled through Winchester and Front Royal, Va., through West Virginia, and to the sparkling little town of Old Town, Md.

I stopped at the Paw Paw park and walked a mile or so. I wanted to photograph the tunnel which formed part of the Chesapeake and Ohio canal, sometimes referred to as the Grand Old Ditch. It was abandoned and never connected the Ohio River but was used to haul coal from the Allegheny Mountains.

I spotted a T-Mobile store in one of the little towns I passed through. I stopped and spoke with the clerk about the issue with my phone the other night. We tried to recreate the problem to no avail. She made a couple of adjustments anyway, and off I rode.

I'd brought along my Nikon D-7200 but hadn't used it much. I had it packed in the left-hand saddlebag, away from the pipes. It was wrapped in a zip lock bag to keep moisture out, but it seemed a pain to retrieve it. I took a few photos at special places but was entertained in different ways to gain quick access to the camera.

It was almost July. In the years gone by, this time of the year would find my family and me on vacation, traveling north from Penns Grove, NJ, to Meadville, Pa. (a 400-mile trip) to enjoy the July 4th family reunion.

There were camping trips in the 60s and 70s. Everyone drank to excess, even the kids and the dog. We'd sit around the campfire and tell stories. Nugget, the Golden Retriever, would sneak up behind people and drink whatever they had in the red Solo cups.

We would fish during the day and collect firewood for that night. One time, when Aunt Bea tried to stand up from her lawn chair, she almost fell into the fire. As her son John tried to help her up from the bushes, she laughed hysterically and shouted, "Leave me the f#@$ alone. I'm peeing."

We all laughed...

Aunt Dot was quiet until she got a few in her, and my mother (the remaining sister) wasn't... More on her another time.

As the years rolled by, we moved the almost week-long party to my cousin John's house. We began setting up to play this new-fangled game called "frisbee golf."

John was an artist. He'd decorated paper plates. We would staple them to broomsticks and hammer them into the ground around the yard. They were all numbered from one to nine. We formed teams, usually brothers against cousins.

As the years passed, family members showed up with their discs in briefcases. We began to see uniforms (tee-shirts) and warming jackets. The competition was becoming fierce, and the shit-slinging was epic. The drunker we got, the louder we got. Usually, the keg was located at the fifth hole—most times near the porch. The family came from all over the U.S., and many of them brought fireworks.

Most would tell you that alcohol and gunpowder do not mix. The Smith family endorsed both with enthusiasm. People from all over Blooming Valley and Saegertown would pull up at the bottom of the hill on the 4th of July to watch the only fireworks show in the area. I never figured out which was better: the fireworks or the drunks.

I guess it had to be the drunks. I remember the only fireworks were when Eric and I were sitting on the roof watching Uncle Ron light up the good stuff. I recall someone put a spinning fire wheel on a post out front. Once lit, that son of a gun came off the post and headed right for drunkards' row. Everyone sitting in lawn chairs scattered, falling over the lawn chairs to save their beverages and their lives. I thought Eric and I would fall off the roof. We laughed so hard.

Those days are long gone now. My cousin John had since passed away, along with his brother Cork. Our mothers, fathers, aunts and uncles, many cousins from my generation, and even my son Nick are gone. I was going home at this memorable time of year, and it seemed so special.

When I neared Cumberland, Md., coming down through the mountains, the bike began to act funny. As I was negotiating a curve, the bike's rear end seemed almost to give way. I found myself drifting around the corners. This could be pretty scary with no place to pull over.

I came to a traffic calming circle. I have no clue why they call it that; it certainly seemed to have the opposite effect on motorists. Then a second one (They were back-to-back.) After the second circle, I stopped. My back tire was flat, and I was in a pretty seedy neighborhood. But it was daytime, and I had some time before it got dark. I made a couple of phone calls to bike shops, but I was told, "This is a metric shop, won't touch it."

I called the Harley shop. They hooked me up with a tow and changed the tire and tube. A couple of hours and 500 dollars later, I was on my way, and I still had just over 100 miles to travel.

Eric and Tara were great people. They had a beautiful family and home. They were very successful and some of the best parents I knew. By the time I pulled up, it was about dark. Eric had a spot for my Harley in the garage, next to his black SUV. The bike and his truck certainly complemented one another. I stayed with them for three days.

At some point, my phone went completely haywire with the green screen thing. Tara was kind. She drove us all over Hell's Half Acre to get my phone fixed. Two different T-Mobile stores were on opposite ends of the city. It took most of the day.

One evening, they took the rest of the family and me and drove us around Pittsburgh. We rode the trolley up the side of Mt. Washington, and we strolled around downtown and saw the old PPG building. It was a wonderful opportunity to get to know them better and take photos.

Because of Covid, Eric was working from home, so we could catch up on the lost years.

As we said goodbye Friday morning and I pulled away, I became sad thinking about his Pop and mine, and the years have gone from sight.

Going north, I headed to Meadville, about a one-and-a-half-hour ride. I took the scenic route remembering the last time I had traveled with my mom and sisters through these parts.

My mother was born to a Baptist minister, John D. Smith, in 1920. He was also a used car salesman, a lady's man, and an entrepreneur who made and sold glue from horses' hooves. He worked in the basement, making the glue in my grandmother's washtub, and would sell it during the Depression.

When my grandfather was a boy, he was best friends with Tom Mix. Tom was a cowboy actor later in life. It was said he was friends with and attended Wyatt Earp's funeral. But growing up in Sharon, Pa., he and my grandfather were best of friends.

One time, they made a deal. My grandfather traded his wagon for Tom's goat. The only issue was that my grandfather had no place to keep a goat. Well, except for inside the vacant house next door. He wasn't aware he needed to feed the goat regularly, so the goat went about doing what goats do; it peeled and ate the wallpaper.

My Great grandmother had no idea this goat was next door. She happened to be in her kitchen doing dishes when she looked out the window and saw this goat standing in the window of the vacant house across from her. She thought she had seen the Devil himself. It startled her so badly that she dropped and broke an armful of dishes. My Grandfather got his ass warmed really good, as the story goes.

Once I arrived in Meadville, I rode around town for a while to reminisce before heading to Carole's. One might think I'd know my way around pretty well. After all, I'd been traveling there for over sixty years. But I got lost just the same.

I wanted to find Aunt Dot's house. It had been in the family for almost 100 years. My mother grew up in that house. As a youngster, she would dig up violets from the ravine in the cemetery and plant them in the yard— much of my family rest in that cemetery. I believe there might be remnants of those violets still at the house. There aren't many changes in those old steel towns up north.

I got to Carole's place; it had been a few years since I had been there. She and I were the same age. We played together as kids, and we'd remained close over the decades.

Once I got settled, I received a message from Tara telling me they were coming up for the weekend. They had a camper at Conneaut Lake and wanted me to bring Carole for a visit that evening. I knew Carole had an art show that weekend near Conneaut Lake. She had to prepare for it and might not be able to get away. I was torn but agreed to try. Carole was more than willing to drive out.

We headed out just before dark. We found more than I had anticipated. Eric's brother CC and their Mom Donna Lu were there. I was so excited! That would be as close as I might ever get to another family reunion. Words cannot express the love my heart felt that night.

We sat around a campfire like we once did, laughing and telling stories. The kids laughed along with us. Our shared experiences from long ago were alive that night for just a little while. I'd hoped it would never end.

Carole and I left late. She got up early and packed for the art show, and I took off to find an AA meeting.

Afterward, I visited other family members, Carole's brother Pete, his son Zeb, and our cousin John Lee. Then I spent Saturday night at Donna Lu's. We covered much ground in the few hours we spent together. She and her late husband gave me refuge when I ran away as a youngster. I stayed with them during the summer months. She and John were great role models. I just wasn't paying attention. It's no wonder her sons are such good parents.

Before I left Florida In June, I had purchased a communication headset for my helmet. It was rather expensive, but I felt it would be a good companion along the way. Not only could I take phone calls. I could also listen to music through Bluetooth.

Sunday afternoon, when Carole returned, we went for a ride. She wore my helmet. There is no helmet law in Pennsylvania, so I could ride without one. I hooked Carole up with good tunes as we rode the backroads at sunset.

She had so much fun we decided to go again in the morning. I carried my helmet down and hung it on the sissy bar, then I set up the phone in its holder and prepared the bike and GPS.

Carole loaded up, and off we roared. However, she'd not seen the helmet sitting on the sissy bar. At some point, it fell off the back. Neither of us noticed it was gone until that night. I was setting things up to leave in the morning and realized the helmet was missing. We spent over an hour looking for it, to no avail, so in the morning, I had to find a bike shop and buy a new helmet without the Sena 30k system.

Riding Northeast

I couldn't leave until I bought a helmet. I rode west toward Conneaut Lake, and I got there just as the motorcycle shop opened. I found a half helmet there that would work. I figured at my pace, my next part of the journey would take me about seven hours or so, and I expected poor weather later in the day.

I took Route 86 north, toward the boroughs of Northeast, Pa., and stopped at a little mom & pop diner along the route, "Davis Country Kitchen." I ordered bacon and eggs. Just a few minutes later, the owner/cook/husband came over to deliver the food that his wife had prepared.

The place had started to clear out when I got there. We exchanged pleasantries, and he inquired where I was headed and where I came from. I told him I was from Florida but "wasn't quite certain where I was headed."

It seemed most folks were enthralled with travel, especially on a motorcycle. The experience was quite different from a car, like rain...

Let's talk about rain. When I'm on a bike, traveling at highway speeds, rain hurts like hell. I'm somewhat protected if I'm behind a windshield, but my knuckles aren't. Regardless of the ambient temperature, it can get cold.

I had pretty good rain gear, but I was soaked anyway, if not from rain, from sweat before long. On one ride before I left home, I got caught in a downpour without rain gear.

The heavy rain usually passes quickly in Florida, so I continued along at 60 mph. When I got home, my legs were dry, as was my torso, but my lower unit (my butt) was still soggy.

It began to pour outside the diner. I hurried out to get the rain gear, but the way it was stowed took much too long to retrieve. I knew I'd need to devise another plan. I already had an issue with this on my way to Asheville.

Back inside, I finished my breakfast. I squared up at the register and stepped into the foyer to don the slicker. It didn't look as though it would clear anytime soon, and it was still raining hard. I forged ahead anyway, pouring rain pelting me and fogging my glasses. Soon enough, it began to clear, just as I started to head east on Route 5, along Lake Erie's edge.

I was taken aback by Northeast Pa. I had heard of this town many times. The area is noted for its wineries and its ability to produce some of the best grapes for winemaking. My favorite grapes are the Concord variety. During my childhood, Mr. Mauser, a neighbor, had decided to rid his yard of his concord grapevines. My other neighbor, Mr. Brantley, built an arbor maybe ten feet wide by fifteen feet long to house those vines. In early fall, the white and blue Concord Grapes were ripe and hung well within our reach. We'd eat them until we were fat as ticks, sick, or both.

The vineyards here grew right up to the bluffs along the edge of Lake Erie. In many places, they were on both sides of the road. I found a park in Westfield with a boat launch and pulled in. I parked the bike, took photos of the area, and found several more breathtaking places along the route.

My favorite was 1964 Lake Rd. There was no pull-off, so I turned and pulled up close to the guardrail and stepped off the bike.

The bluffs wrapped around in both directions of the cove. It seemed like I'd found a hole in the sky; the rain fell all around me. The wind blew from the west, so I just followed it. I tried to be alert for the special places to catch another glimpse of God's handiwork, and this was one of them.

I was headed to Marion, NY, to see Mike and his wife, Janine, just south of Sodus Point, which is on the lake. Mike and I worked together from about 1983 on. We were pipefitters/welders.

The first job we worked on together was at Monsanto. I had made a field weld for Mike on a 3" pipe. It was difficult, just a few inches off the ground. Being in a good position was key, so Mike lay on the ground. He had to hold his head in a position that gave him cramps in his neck. I kneeled beside him and slid my knee under his head because I could see him struggle to get comfortable. He felt my knee, and it startled him. He jumped and looked at me with scolding eyes. But once I explained myself, Mike knew he was in good hands and went on to finish the weld. That began a lifelong friendship built on trust.

There are some people in life you just click with, like Yin and Yang. We were just that way. Mike is a brilliant guy. His sense of humor and witty sarcasm brought laughs to every job. He and Janine had moved here from Jersey ten to fifteen years ago. This was my second visit.

When I pulled in, Mike greeted me with a hug. I unpacked the bike, and he showed me to my room. On the dresser was a high-powered rifle with a scope and bipod. The window was open, and the screen was sitting on the floor. Mike informed me the gun was locked and loaded, and should I see a groundhog by his barn, I was to shoot it.

Mike had a large shop in the back, where he built what we'd come to know as "doodads." Anything built in Mike's shop could be construed as a "doodad." It might be a kiln, a bicycle part, a baffle, or something for a tractor or a boiler, but while there, it was a doodad. Mike would build or fix it.

He had a collection of old bicycles; a 1932 Schwinn, a mid-'60s Japanese muscle bike called a Skyway, and at least one other one that he built for his son to ride in a parade back in the '80s or '90s. They have two children, who are both very successful. Janine is retired from the school system. She stays busy volunteering with local activities. Mike still works almost full-time and probably always will.

He and I changed the fluids in my Harley while I was there. It was at the 10,000-mile mark, and it just so happened Mike had all the oil and O-rings we needed. He even had a filter.

Mike knows his way around bikes. He once built a chopper from the ground up. He and Joe (who you'll meet later) built a jig that would enable them to create multiple hardtail frames identically. They welded tubing together using the jig to keep everything aligned. The motor, the back wheel, and the tree for the front forks all needed to line up. They won trophies for one of the bikes they built.

I have always admired his talent. I only recall one time that he made a mistake. He was pouring a new driveway. We had a "new driveway cement pouring party." Some of us were under the influence of something. We stood there grinning from ear to ear when the truck showed up. Shrooms will do that.

The driver informed Mike that we probably wouldn't have enough concrete. It turned out that Mike miscalculated how much would be needed for the pour. We decided to improvise. Mike had lots of car parts, like starters, alternators, and other things that would make the driveway a little stronger and take up space. We threw in all kinds of stuff, like mufflers, a tailpipe, and even some tools into the pour. We laughed and fell and just had a great time. I don't know who owns that house now, but they're in for some surprises if they take that driveway up.

Mike had always been generous with his time, talent, and good fortune. We had many good times together over the years. I appreciate Janine and Mike and the impact they'd had on my life.

I fixed dinner one night. I think it was my mom's chicken and dumplings. (Mom called it pot pie). I also made a cheesecake.

I wanted to leave the smallest footprint possible at each place I stayed. I packed my pillow and towel. I also packed several things I didn't need. The T-bag was beginning to tear when I cinched it up. I wasn't sure it would make the entire trip. I planned on thinning the load when I got to Jersey. I needed to eliminate the expandable part of the bag that was failing because I couldn't zip it shut with the extra clothes I'd brought. I knew I could make do with less.

Janine was involved with the town's upcoming Apple Blossom Festival, and somehow Mike got "volunteered" to help organize and house the golf carts used for officials. I rode with him into Williams. They have a partnership in the old Grange Hall there.

It was a beautiful historic building full of antiquities. They'd put extensive work into the building to rehab it, and now they let space out to local artisans.

The night before I left, when Janine returned to the house from the Grange, she presented me with a T-shirt. It was gray with white lettering, "I Have a Checkered Past," and checkered flags on the front. I loved it! I'd received many compliments on it along the road. I certainly had a checkered past, and those two knew it.

When I left Saturday morning, I had mixed emotions. We never know when we'll say goodbye for the last time. But I was excited to begin the next leg of this journey. I was going to see my sister soon.

The sky was gray, the air damp and cool. As I rode south, it seemed it would rain. I wasn't going to let the weather dampen my mood.

Southeast Bound

I headed south on 21, east to 14, and south again along beautiful Cayuga Lake. The views of the lake would come and go.

The sky began to darken. I pulled off the road and put on the slicker gear. I had folded and kept it just under the bungee cords that wrapped the entire T bag. However, the sky soon cleared, and it didn't rain.

I stopped several times to take photographs, once at Taughannock Falls State Park. I passed through Ithaca, Slaterville Springs, Whitney Point, and a few other little towns, each with its own charm. How nice it would be to spend a few days in this area.

Bethel Woods was 220 miles from Marion, about seven riding hours. (I drive slowly and lollygag.)

As I pulled into the parking lot on Herd Road at The Woodstock Memorial, I found one spot available for my bike. I was excited to be there again.

I opened the Saddlebag and grabbed the Nikon and began shooting immediately. The camera had always been something of a security blanket for me over the years. It was an ice breaker, as well. I bought my first Digital D-50 around 2006. Shortly after that, I bought my first desktop to view, edit and maintain the pictures I took.

Several people sat around a picnic table chatting, and a few had lanyards that hung around their necks. It was an official badge: "The Museum at Bethel Woods Center for the Arts." Below was the wearer's name and the words... "Festival Attendant."

Bobbi Ercoline, an attractive woman, introduced herself, her husband Nick, and Mayor Mike Malone. All wore similar identification. Like most folks my age who could not attend the original Woodstock, I was enthralled with the festival and those who attended or tried to. Bess, my wife's mother, was from Newton, N.J., just a couple of hours south, but got stranded just twenty miles away.

Countless friends had attended, and the stories varied, but all were amazing.

I'd been there a couple of years before with my daughter Lorian when she was almost fifteen. She knew nothing of Woodstock. We left that morning from New York City, East Village. We rented a flat while we explored the city. I had the Woodstock Album on my phone, and we listened to it in its entirety. I stopped the music just before Santana's "Soul Sacrifice." I brought up a YouTube video of an interview with Carlos Santana giving the background info on their manager Bill Graham prior to the Festival; and how he groomed them for larger and larger venues, each time taking a chunk of the audience with them.

By the time the band got to Woodstock, they were not afraid of the crowds. Carlos, thinking he had at least twelve hours to go before they would perform, took LSD. He was wrong. It was a great story. He talked about his guitar coming alive and the faces he made.

I listened while she watched the live Woodstock version of "Soul Sacrifice" as we drove. We laughed as we traveled the same back roads that many kids took way back then. The rest of the album played, and I explained the best I could what times were like back in 1969. When we entered the Museum, I was taken aback by the photos, the memorabilia, and the artifacts. I was in a rush because I had convinced myself Lorian was humoring me and thought she would soon tire of this display and probably would want to leave. Instead, to my surprise, she came running out of the psychedelic bus and grabbed me by the hand. She pulled me back inside, where we were seated, and watched a video. She was certainly enamored by all this Hippie stuff.

We went through the entire place. At one point, I found part of the PA system, which in 1969 was perched on the scaffolding on either side of the stage. I believe there were eight altogether. I stood alongside the PA, touching it gently with my hands, knowing Jimi Hendrix's guitar wailed the "Star Spangled Banner" through its speakers. A fella walked into the room and looked at me oddly as I smilingly said, "You can still feel the magic." And you could.

I sat across from Bobbi, listening to her and Nick tell the story of how they almost didn't go. $18 was quite a bit of money back then, with the minimum wage at $1.30 an hour. When they heard the gates open, they took his mother's 1965 Chevrolet Impala Station Wagon and headed out. They lived an hour or so away.

They approached a roadblock secured by State police. The officer instructed the motorcycle driver in front of them to turn around and go home. He completely disregarded the officer and proceeded to jump the curb and cut across a cornfield. Bobbi and Nick followed the motorcyclist in the station wagon.

While telling the story, a woman approached Bobbi and asked, "How'd they find you? How'd they know it was you?"

As I pondered her question, I looked at the woman behind me (with furrowed brow). Just then, I realized I had been talking to the iconic couple on the album cover, wrapped in the quilted blanket.

There are no words to describe what I felt at that precise moment. I had been chatting with them for over twenty minutes and never uttered a word about it. I felt as though I was in the presence of royalty.

We had lots of questions about their favorite moments and most memorable songs. I asked where the people bathed. Bobbi pointed up the hill and told me, "The large pond up behind those houses."

She asked, "Why?"

I explained that I considered that "holy water." When I was there last time, I failed to collect some. This was the biggest reason I returned.

She smiled, saying, "I've never heard it called that, but I believe you're right.".

I stayed with them for another hour before riding over to collect some water. But first, I went through the museum. They had changed the exhibit from my prior visit. Today, it would be a collection of early posters; some were blacklight posters. The PA was still there but behind ropes to protect it from people who might get fingerprints on it. Who would do that?

I left the museum and rode up the hill to where I could see the pond behind the houses. There was a small lane that led back as maybe a canoe ramp. I walked around with a water bottle, reached under the gate, and filled it up. Later, I shipped the bottle back to Florida. Once I returned home, I ordered tiny flasks with corks.

I've been filling these up with just a few drops and handing them out to friends ever since.

I still had a couple of hours to travel to an Airbnb in Scranton, so I said my goodbyes and headed south. At some point, I needed to get the address and stopped to contact the homeowner at the Airbnb, to no avail. After several failed attempts, I called Airbnb. I was told that my request to rent was denied. Everything else was much more than I was willing to part with. Typically, I try to find a room to share (hostel), it's much cheaper, and I get to meet other travelers.

I decided to abandon the Airbnb since I couldn't stay there anyway and head to Collingswood, N.J., to see my nephew, Jeff. With over 180 miles to travel yet, that translated into a late night for me.

While winding my way through the Catskills, I caught peeks of the Delaware River several times. I grew up next to this body of water. I wondered if perhaps I had seen these same water molecules at some other poignant time in my life.

I watched a boy drown when I was twelve. I was fishing at the old Wilson Line pier in Penns Grove. He was swimming with friends when he got caught in the current. He was the same age as I was at the time. I'd fished these waters most of my life. I have enough memories that I could write a book about those times.

I came through Delaware State Park in New York. Another thing about riding a motorcycle instead of driving a car is the scents encountered. For most people, travel consists of a beginning point and a destination. For me, the fabric of travel contained much more, especially on a motorcycle –Temperature changes going through valleys and shady areas, scents, and sights along the way. Hidden things we might never see traveling at highway speeds flowing with traffic.

There in the Catskills, the pine smell was intoxicating. It reminded me of the Christmas trees of long ago. I pulled off into a parking area as I was getting tired. I parked the bike and retired against the front wheel. My naps lasted about 10-20 minutes, but they're all I need to continue safely. Somehow, I crossed the Delaware River a few more times.

Just before dusk, I found myself at the Delaware Water Gap. I remembered a trip there with my sister Lori, her husband Tony, and my girlfriend Jacque. We camped at Ringing Rocks Campground. Tony and I got smashed.

We drove to a remote spot to light a quarter stick, commonly called an M-80. It was completely dark out there. We lit the firecracker and tossed it about ten feet. When that thing exploded, the report was extremely loud, much louder than expected. The flash was so bright it blinded us. We panicked. We were certain someone would come looking to see what that explosion was. We turned to run to the car and crashed into each other, falling to the ground. We just laid on the ground laughing so hard we couldn't get up.

When we finally got back to the campsite, my sister wore a blonde bombshell wig with a naughty red nighty. She got very provocative with her husband. Downright slutty, in fact. We had so much fun that weekend. I'd always liked those spur-of-the-moment get-aways.

The closer I got to my destination, the worse the roads became. I hit one pothole north of Philly on Route13, where I thought, I would get ejected from the bike. I'll never understand why Google took me back and forth over the river, but I got to see it plenty of times from different angles.

I pulled into Jeff's place a little after 10 pm. He had a motorcycle cabana set up for me along the street to keep the bike safer and dry.

Jeff gave me a huge hug. His son, Little Jeff, was there, too. I hadn't seen him in over twenty-five years.

They helped me unload the bike and carry everything up to the house.

He is seven years my junior. Jeff is more like a little brother to me than a nephew. His father, Pat, died suddenly of heart failure at only thirty-three years old. I so loved his dad. Everyone did. Pat was the older brother I'd always wanted. He was a handsome guy. Both his parents were Italian.

Times were different in 1962. My Mother considered my sister and Pat to be in an interracial relationship and was against the marriage. But it wasn't long before my mother fell in love with Pat. His untimely death echoed across the universe. I still can hear his mother, Philomena's wails. We all cried, but not like she did. There is no pain like that of losing a child.

I always felt a need to nurture those two boys, Jeff and his brother Tim. Their fathers, brothers, and sister took even better care of them than I did. When Tim moved to California in 1990, Jeff and I spent more and more time together. We even shared an apartment at one point.

The apartment complex Jeff manages now had a late July 4th cookout. We don't typically see cookouts in Florida; it's too damn hot. I was tickled to join in and help set up. I had a great time with the tenants. Most of them were my age or older.

I think it was before that party that Jeff and I made our way to Salem to see my sister Lori in the nursing home. This was just over a year into the Covid pandemic. We were required to refrain from touching and wore masks. They sat Lori at the end of a table, with a plexiglass panel between us.

The nurses drew the curtain, and Lori looked over at Jeff with a smile, then at me, and her mouth dropped open, and her eyes lit up. She said, "David!"

I cried and pulled my mask away. I made my way around the table and held my sister. We kissed and embraced for a long time. Jeff joined us.

My sister had two aneurysms about ten years ago that left her with some brain damage. She couldn't be alone, so I brought her to Florida with me when her second husband passed away. Just a few weeks later, we lost my closest sibling, Julie. She and Lori were best friends, as well as sisters.

A year later, we took Lori on vacation to Jersey. Within a day of arriving, she got sick. She was hospitalized, then placed in a nursing facility that she hasn't been able to leave for more than a couple of hours since. I'd been trying to see Lori since before covid began. She was in lockdown most of the time. Even her son had to wave to her from outside the building. That was not a life worth living; in my estimation, if you cannot touch and be with the ones you love.

We were permitted a half-hour with Lori. We'd brought her a Hoagie and a coke. Jeff made her pizzelles.

After we left, we stopped at a produce stand along Route 45 to grab tomatoes and corn. Jersey produces some of the best tomatoes available anywhere.

Jeff and I went back to see Lori a few more times while I was there. On the way to the nursing home, we stopped at Cowtown, affectionately referred to as the Sharpstown Mall, on old Route 40. There was a weekly Rodeo on Saturday nights during the summer months.

The adjacent buildings housed vendors who sold clothing, wares, toiletries, food, and more. It was open Tuesdays and Saturdays. The hot peanuts were always a great investment, and the Amish meats were amazing.

Outside was a flea market, with tools and just about anything one could want. I'd never been to the rodeo in all the years that I lived less than ten miles away. It was probably a good thing. I think when I was young, I considered myself bulletproof. I'd have probably gotten really stupid and real hurt at the rodeo.

***

I got a call from my old friends Kim and Nancy. I was the best man at their wedding. I'd known Kim since the 6th grade, and Nancy lived down the street from me as a kid. They eloped to Elkton, Maryland, many years ago. They invited me to visit with them at their daughter's new home. I teased them a little.

Kim and Nancy had sold the home they had owned for almost forty years. The sale went so quickly they hadn't had time to find something suitable, so they temporarily moved in with their youngest daughter Becca. I suggested that Nancy had solved the age-old riddle of "Empty Nest Syndrome" by moving in with the kids.

I first traveled to Becca's, but Nancy and Kim needed to tend to a few things at their son Jared's house. He was on vacation. We got together for a BBQ at his place later that day anyway. We played around in the pool and caught up while cooking burgers and hot dogs. We even had fresh corn.

I was getting ready to shove off when a heck of a storm came through. The thunder was deafening. A lightning bolt hit extremely close and scared all three of us. We laughed, but Nancy hauled ass in the house.

Kim and I laughed about another time we faced this stuff, in his '66 mustang with a 3-on-the-tree shifter. We sat along the Delaware River, watching a storm. We were probably high on reefer or something when a bolt of lightning "appeared" to hit the front of the car. I can still see us screaming and almost jumping into each other's laps. We were maybe eighteen.

We decided to stay put for the night at Jared's. The weather didn't let up much, and I was on the bike. I got up before 6 am and left quietly. The garage was open, so I pushed the bike out to not wake them. I locked everything up, pushed the bike down the driveway, fired it up, and left. I got about ten minutes away and realized I had no helmet on. How the hell does that happen?

Jersey has a helmet law, and the troopers travel Route 45 frequently, so I spun around and headed back. Halfway there, I realized I'd locked everything. I pulled into the driveway and walked around the garage. Luckily, I found a window on the side that was open. I crawled inside, got my lid, and left. Like the first time, I don't think I woke anyone else up as I made my second getaway.

I had planned to visit several old friends while I was home. I wanted to catch a couple of AA meetings, hit the Jersey Shore, spend time at Wildwood by the Sea, and get some of Mack's pizza. It's the best there is!

There were other special places I liked to visit. One was the softball fields on Route 130 in Carneys Point. On May 30, 1978, I worked for the Salem County Bridge Department. We were tasked with building the baseball fields. The Department of Defense donated the property. Time was running out to begin construction, and the land would be appropriated somewhere else. I was welding one of the backstops when I heard a lot of commotion. My boss was whistling, and I heard people screaming. I flipped up my welding hood and looked over my shoulder to see my extremely pregnant wife. I could tell she was in labor.

I jumped down from the top platform, about twelve feet, tossing gloves, the welding hood, and my leathers as I ran toward my wife and her mother. We jumped in the '71 Ford pickup and headed toward the hospital in Delaware. Now, I had a 1969 Dodge Monaco with a 383 cubic inch motor that would flat out fly. I had told both women that if Melody went into labor, to drive my car. It was a boat. It handled great. It was comfortable and fast. "Just drive to the hospital," I said.

But no! My mother-in-law was nervous driving my car, so they brought the truck.

The truck spat and sputtered. I couldn't get it to go much faster than fifteen miles per hour, but somehow, we managed to get to the local volunteer fire department. I asked for an ambulance. We were still ten minutes from the bridge that would take us to Delaware from New Jersey. Melody had picked one of a few female OBGYNs in the area, but her practice was across the river in Delaware.

The big siren on top of the station sounded loud enough, so anyone within a few miles knew that help was needed, and a few guys came running in from the neighborhood. Big guys, with flannel shirts and ball caps. They looked like they had just cut out of a softball game. They put Melody in the back of the ambulance, I rode shotgun, and off we went.

My young bride was terrified, in active labor and in the hands of strangers. I'm sure she assumed they were great at putting out fires, but she wasn't in the least interested in them delivering our baby. I think one fellow still had orange fingers from eating Cheetos.

Getting to the right hospital took several attempts. We pulled into the first hospital, and a sign out in front declared that Emergency was at a different facility. We tried to rush Melody to that hospital. However, none of us knew our way around Wilmington, so we drove in circles with the lights flashing and the siren blaring. We finally pulled into the emergency room only to discover we had just left the correct hospital, which was for maternity.

The staff took my extremely modest wife into the Emergency Room to take a look. They passed that poor woman around like the collection plate on Sunday morning. They said she was fine and sent us off to find the first hospital. We only got a little lost this time, and we made it with at least four minutes or so to spare.

Back then, it wasn't that popular for the husband to join in the delivery room, but join I did. Now, I had no trouble with the spilling of my blood. I'd seen it more than a few times in some quantity. But hers; that was a different thing. I almost passed out. I vaguely recall the doctors ordering someone to get me out of there. The lights still go out every time.

Nick had bilirubin. I felt so powerless seeing him naked in that incubator with ultraviolet lights and his eyes covered.

I took time to ride out to the old Route 322, a concrete highway that leads to what was once the Bridgeport-Chester Ferry. I have several memories there. My sister Julie and I had driven Pop's' Mopar out to ride the ferry the last night it was in operation. It was ten cents for pedestrians.

We parked the car and rode back and forth a few times. I took my young bride out there once after it closed. I found a pot plant and a pretty good-sized one, too. We were driving a buddy's 1972 MG. I got a little paranoid with that plant in the back seat of a convertible, but we made it home without incident.

Y'know, just the other night, a fella commented that I had big balls to take a trip like this by myself, but as I write some of these stories, I'm starting to think I might be just a little stupid.

I had called a couple of friends, Tom and Norma. I thought things might be a little cramped at Jeff's and asked if they'd have room. I met these folks many years ago. My first encounter was in their backyard. They were having a cookout. Horseshoes was the game, and I was invited. I'd never played until now.

Tom had set his old motorcycle up to use the headlight to light up the pits. My first shot missed terribly, but my second toss was right through that headlight. Game Over. That was how it started, and for some reason, they kept inviting me back. We began playing softball on Sundays at the local little league field in Woodstown.

One fella, Craig, had a new 1987 Ford Ranger. He lined the bed with plastic and filled it with water from the garden hose. He'd float in an inner tube, drink a cold beer and smoke a doobie between innings.

We snuck up and opened the tailgate. After being asked not to play there anymore, we moved to a field in a more remote location, in Alloway.

Norma's sister Patty was pitching, and I was at bat. I crushed a line drive right back at Patty that hit her in the pubic bone. She dropped to her knees as I continued around first base. I was called to go back to first. Finally, Patty got her composure after several minutes of excruciating pain. As she regained her position on the mound, my son Nick stepped up to the plate. Taking the lead to first base, I called out to Nick as I clapped, "C'mon, Nick! Hit it in the same hole!"

Patty chased me all over that ball field. She threw the ball, then her glove. I laughed so hard I couldn't run.

We had so many good times together over the years. I was hoping to stay with them for a couple of nights. I ran out of time, but I did get to briefly visit Tom twice while I was there.

I always like to attend some recovery meetings while traveling, especially near my old hometown. I had no idea how long I'd be there, so I figured I'd get to something sooner rather than later.

The stretch of I-295 between Collingswood and Penns Grove was the most efficient route to take, even though I wanted to avoid highways. The traffic any other way was worse. I made a 7 am meeting a couple of times.

After one of the meetings, I spoke with a fella we'll call John. He inquired as to whether I had an older brother. I said, "No."

When he told me his last name, I vaguely recognized it and asked if he knew a man we'll call Charlie.

His face lit up, and he nodded and said, "Yes, we've been friends a long time!"

I continued, "Did you, he and a couple of other guys leave TK's bar and drive to a Phillies game, leave halfway through to go to a strip joint; then go driving through Philly at 100 plus mph into Jersey and get thrown out of the seediest strip joint ever?"

John was amazed that I knew the whole story, what kind of car, and which bar. He asked how I knew.

I said, "I was driving! And I'm the reason we got kicked out of the strip joint."

We laughed some, but we both also realized retrospectively how lucky we were to be still alive and not have hurt anyone.

That escapade was 1987. I often reflect on how much my life had changed from who I was back then. I made the trip down there a couple more times for more meetings, all time well spent.

Katie and I spoke on the phone, but it was always difficult for us to chat about any goings-on. At some point, she suggested I not return to Florida until

September. She said by then, she would have a place and be moved.

Jeff, my nephew, took a couple of days off to travel with me to Wildwood. Kim and Nancy met us there, on the beach. The beaches in the Wildwoods vary in width. It was a quarter mile from the boardwalk to the water's edge in some places. Others were quite narrow.

We sat in the sun, listening to the music of the pounding surf, the laughing gulls, and children playing. This is the same song that one hears at every beach, no matter where it is.

The three guys, Kim, Jeff, and I, jumped in the ocean. One of my favorite things to do is body surfing. Well, there were a bunch of young fellas there with the boogie boards, trying to catch a wave. Here came three old, fat guys, out there with no boards, catching waves and riding them up until we'd "belly out" or run aground. Those kids just couldn't figure it out.

We had a blast. I looked them right in the eye before I'd catch a wave, point at the wave, give a thumbs up, and go. When I stood up at the end of a good run, I looked back and threw another thumbs up in their direction and headed out to catch another.

Toward the end of the day, an old flame showed up. Her family had a condo there. Debbie and I dated when I was sixteen, I think. She and her sister Sherrie came to hang with us. They were both heartthrobs. They were still beautiful women.

I once thumbed it, also known as hitchhiking to the uninitiated, through a blizzard to their house, about fifteen miles from where I lived. There weren't too many cars, so I walked much of the way to see her. Something about that girl drove me to do crazy things to see her.

She reminded me of a New Years' party we attended, and she had a little too much to drink. She got sick. She told me I held her hair while she threw up and was a complete gentleman. So for those who know me and think I'm a total pig… see there; I was nice once! Well, she was pretty inebriated. Maybe she had the wrong guy.

After leaving the beach, we walked on the boardwalk to get Mack's pizza. It's the best pie I'd ever had. I measure every other pizza against this one. Most don't come close.

We came here on vacation for two weeks every year when I was a kid. We rented a place from a couple that had a set of twin sons, Bobbie and Richie. They would shine shoes on the boardwalk. Back then, no one wore sneakers, except for children. Everyone wore leather shoes.

They began taking me with them. I would charge fifteen cents or twenty-five for a half-assed spit shine. That's where I would spit on your shoes and take your quarter. I was short and cute, so I got away with it. Last year, I donated my shoeshine box to the City of Wildwood Historical Society. It's on display, I'm told.

I had time to visit a few more friends. I made a couple of trips to Delaware, one of them to see my old friend Patty. We were neighbors for seventeen years. We played together as kids. We went trick or treating together, and her older brother, Steve, was probably my first best friend.

Steve and I pushed and pulled each other around in wagons. One of our favorite pastimes was climbing to the top of a tree in the woods and having someone chop it down. They fall in a kind of slow motion. We built forts, and we argued over whose dad could beat up whose dad. Once, I threw a stone at Steve. He ducked, and the stone flew past his head right through my old man's back window. I hollered, "What'd ya duck for?"

I can still hear Steve laughing.

I got to Patty's about noon. Like many grandparents, Patty was raising her grandchildren. Her mother, who was in her 90s, was there. She drove every day and let no grass grow under her feet. We shared plenty of stories and caught up on the lost years. Patty and I shared lots of memories.

She made us lunch. She's an awesome cook. I see plenty of her amazing recipes on social media.

The second place I stopped was to see Joe. We met at work. He and I hung out after work and partied together. We had several common friends. Joe had, at that time, recently acquired a DUI after a car wreck. He was awaiting a court date, so we partied while we could. Joe was sentenced to a treatment facility for thirty days. I vaguely remember visiting him there. Joe came out and never drank again.

When I left my first wife in 1988, I quit my job and moved to Florida. Things didn't go as planned there, so in January of '89, I tried to move back. But she didn't want me, nor did my kids. It wasn't a marriage; it was more of a hostage situation. I was abusive physically and emotionally. I didn't want my wife to work. Deep inside, I was terrified that she would meet someone else and leave me. Like most drunks, I felt I didn't measure up.

When they rejected my return, I wanted to be a victim and be butt hurt. But the truth was, they were making a sound decision to keep a mean, abusive drunk like me out of their lives. I had no place to go, so I called

Joe. He and I had been in touch, and he let me stay there as long as I followed a few rules. I did for a time, but at one point, bringing booze home was more important than having a home, so I had to leave.

It was eight years later that I got sober. You see, I knew AA worked. I saw it work in Joe's life. I watched his whole life turn around. That scared me, not drinking. Joe saved my life and probably didn't know it.

I had some things to tell him, so we sat for several hours. His wife of many years joined us, and one of his daughters stopped by. He is a true example of the positive changes that can happen to a hopeless drunk. Later, our conversation turned to bikes. He owned a couple of Harleys and one old Norton Commando he had restored. I left with a full heart.

After I visited with Joe, I reached out to a couple of other folks. Two friends live separately in a senior citizen's building. I stopped by and called them, but neither answered. Later, Jacque called me back. I asked if she was up for a motorcycle ride, and she said, "Yeah, sure."

She had ridden with me years ago. I drove over to pick her up and loading her onto the bike was interesting. Being a senior citizen, she couldn't climb on behind me. I had to grab her foot, lift her leg over the bike, walk around the other side, grab her other thigh, and heave her onto the seat. I then mounted the bike in front of her, and off we went.

First, we rode past the house that we once lived in together. The thoughts of how we once were so in love came to mind and how that was destroyed by alcoholism—the fights and the constant chaos that plagued us. In the beginning, I swore to myself that I would not let booze get the upper hand. But it had its way with me and my life without my permission.

We rode through Salem out into Elsinboro, to Oakwood beach. I tried to find roads that were not too rugged. The back seat on that bike was not very forgiving on the backside. We stopped at Hudocks for a bite to eat and a milkshake (the best money can buy.)

A family stopped at the table next to us. The husband commented on my bike and asked if we had driven from Florida. We explained the story to them and that today was Jacque's maiden voyage on the back. I warned them, "they might not wanna watch," but "please, don't laugh at our exit."

The two of us older folks would soon attempt to mount up and drive away. We were all cracking up as we left.

I made a second trip a few days later to see Jacque. I wanted to see her boys. It had been well over twenty-five years since I had spoken with either of them, and I had some amends to make. We rode to Michael's first, then to David's. It was good to see them. Both were very gracious and hugged me as we left. It was a somber ride home, reflecting on so many things as we rode.

I dropped her off and drove to another friend's house in Pennsville. Deb invited me to join her at the Salem County Sportsman's Club. I had been a member there until I moved to Florida in 1997.

It was an amazing facility, with beautiful Lake Hudson and its swim area as its centerpiece. Behind it was the clubhouse, with two fireplaces. One was outside with a deck. A newer bathhouse had been added to the west of the clubhouse, with an apartment above. Southeast of the lake was the gun range, trap and skeet range, and archery range. Beyond that was the campground and boat dock on the Salem River.

This place was so beautiful in the winter months as the snow fell, and it was pretty much unvisited. But during the summer, I spent many hours over the years in various boats on this river, fishing for bass. My older boys, Dave and Nick, camped there with me every year.

One year on Friday afternoon, we were setting up for the weekend. We were watching one of the other fathers and his children taking Carlos's first Jon boat on its maiden voyage. Those were always so fun to watch. He had a trolling motor mounted on the bow. His boys were also in the front of the boat.

Carlos was proud of his new purchase and was showing it off. He sat in the back with his foot controls. He was right in front of the dock, with a priceless smile, when he "threw the juice" to that powerful motor. But instead of taking off, it sucked the front of the Jon boat underwater. His boys and fishing gear floated off. From the dock, the crowd cheered as we gave Carlos a standing ovation.

Deb and I spent a few hours floating around on the lake, talking to some of her friends and chatting. Later, she had invited her folks over for dinner, so we could all catch up.

Her family and I go back some years. I was dating her best friend. Her name was also Debbie. I was fifteen or sixteen at the time. We had caught a ride out to "Lost Lake;" it was late spring, and graduation parties were the norm at those places. Deb's boyfriend, Wayne, was there as well.

The four of us walked around the lake, but when we returned, everyone was gone, and we were left behind, in the middle of nowhere (I guess that's why they call it Lost Lake). We walked home. Deb was late, which did not bode well. Once we got to a paved road, I put my thumb out whenever a car passed. Finally, a man named Kevin picked us up in his truck. Debbie and I rode up front, Wayne, and Deb in the back.

Now here's the back story from her dad. I never heard this side of it until we had dinner with them that night. Deb told her folks she was going to walk down to the river that evening. Her father went looking for her, but she wasn't there. He was already upset. Add to the fact she was late (if you can imagine that). He returned home and crouched in his car, waiting for her to return. He had a couple of beers and was probably pretty angry. I'm sure that stewing in the backseat of a car, imagining the worst, helped his foul mood.

As we pulled up, he came out of nowhere. Deb jumped out of the back of the truck with Wayne, and her father chased Wayne around the truck. Wayne feared for his life; this guy was no joke. An ex-Marine, I think, and he wanted blood. I stepped from the cab as he went past to calm him down. Lousy decision on my part; I got hit. As he chased Wayne, the good Samaritan Kevin said, "Hey! you can't do that."

POW! He got popped in the face.

Wayne cleared the bed of the truck, I jumped up front with Kevin, and off we went.

We got a way down the road, and we stopped to let Wayne up front. Kevin wanted to know who the guy was.

I gave up the last name. He thought for a minute, turned the damn truck around, and headed back.

I thought, *Oh shit*! *This isn't going to end well.*

We pulled up to the house, and he walked up and knocked on the door and stepped inside. It turned out Deb's brother worked for Kevin. A few minutes later, Wayne and I were invited in for hot chocolate and cookies.

Kevin left, and we stayed for a while. Then, I think, we hitchhiked home (I don't remember, that thump on the head was pretty hard).

The rest of the back-story goes like this:

On his way home, Kevin got pulled over by the state police. His eyes bloodshot, the officer gave him a ticket for driving under the influence. Things were different back then. Kevin tried to explain, but the officer said, "Tell it to the judge."

A day or so later, Kevin called Deb's father and asked him to go to court with him. Mr. B agreed. Kevin pleaded not guilty and said he had been punched in the face, and that was why his eyes were bloodshot. He called his witness. Mr. B had his uniform on; he worked as a supervisor for the NJ Turnpike Commission. As Mr. B explained the whole story to the court, the judge hung his head, shaking it back and forth. He grabbed the gavel. "Dismissed."

We sat around Deb's kitchen table that night, laughing so hard. Her husband Rob and I had known each other for many years, but tonight, we became friends. My family got a little bigger.

Jeff took a day off, and we picked up chicken backs, loaded his crab traps, and headed to Ft. Mott to catch a few blue claw crabs. My oldest and one of my dearest friends, Jim, met us there. It was his father who gave up the grape vineyards to my neighbor.

The crabbing was kind of slow, so I arranged to take the shuttle to Ft. Delaware at Pea Patch Island, and off we went. This fort was built during the Civil War and housed tens of thousands of confederate soldiers. Over 2,500 of them died there. They have re-enactments and people dressed to the era. Historians were available to answer questions. They were especially good at getting folks to participate in fun discussions. It's a great place for children.

We caught the last ferry back and decided to roam around Ft. Mott. A golf cart provided us with transportation to the museum. Inside, we found artifacts, maps, cannonballs, and a 60" concave mirror from a lighthouse. I remembered seeing it when I worked there in the summer of 1973.

We strolled outside and saw a couple of people standing below the Lookout Tower. It looked fresh and clean, not decaying, and falling apart as I remembered it. I asked the Fort Historian if it was open, but he answered, "No, we just refinished it. We're awaiting the decking plates for the floor above."

I asked about the renovations to it, and he filled me in. The top was taken off and set on a flatbed. It was sent out to have it cloned. They used rivets, not welding; the glass panels on the roof were manufactured in Millville; they had to use a standard chicken wire sandwiched between two layers of glass instead of the twisted chicken wire in the original top. They even had to have a couple of the cast iron stair treads cast to match the broken ones. The towers were used in triangulation to adjust cannon fire toward enemy ships. A phone system connected the second tower at Fort Mott (not yet restored) and a tower at Pea Patch Island.

I told the historian I had worked there as a young adult. He asked questions about the goings-on then, who my boss was and what the place was like. I answered all that I could and told him a few stories about the family that lived in the old officer quarters. He took notes as I talked.

We finished up, and I thanked him. He stopped me and said, "C'mon."

He reached for his belt and removed the keys as he motioned me to follow him. He unlocked the gate and took us up the freshly restored tower. I climbed those stairs one by one, feeling like royalty.

The last time I made this ascent, I was a teenager. My parents, sister, brother-in-law, and almost all the people I loved were still alive. The world was a different place.

As we entered the structure, I noticed that everything was brand new. A restored telephone hung on the wall. Its bell rang just like it was new. You could see a telephone pole in Delaware through the transit, about 2.7 miles away. The historian explained that even the light switches were like the original and that a 3D printer was used to make these. He gave us a demonstration of how the phone worked. We stayed for about ten minutes. Then we climbed back down.

We left the park and headed toward Carney's Point. We went to the Roman Pantry to order Cheesesteaks. They're some of the best in the area. A large, autographed poster of a hometown boy, Bruce

Willis, was on the wall. Whenever he was in town or nearby, he'll stop and order food. Jim, who was with us, had original 8mm movies of Bruce that he had taken back in the early '70s. Jim had movies of all of us doing dumb kid shit.

I've got forty years of history there in the Delaware Valley. I moved to Florida in January of 1997. Going home to a borough that once thrived and was now boarded up was very strange. Sometimes, it felt as if it was someone else's life here, and I guess, in a way, that's accurate. I was drinking; a Doctor Jekyll/Mr. Hyde. I'm no longer that fella. I just have all his memories.

I connected with my brother-in-law, my sister Julie's widower. I rode out to his mom's house, she lived in Aldine, N.J., and we talked for a few hours about all the life changes each of us had endured.

Then we rode over to Homer's place, where the secret car was kept. You see, there is an old Chevrolet in a barn. It's a two-seater. It's a little unclear who exactly owns it, but, as the story goes, if the right woman found out about this automobile, there would be hell to pay.

Most of us guys were only allowed to have so many toys. We needed to be clever, so storing toys at a buddy's house, well, that was clever.

Byron is a fun guy to hang out with; he's almost as perverted as I am. We yucked it up every time we got together. See, I've always been a dirty old man. I just haven't always been old. Homer fit right in and reminded me of Sam Elliot. We sat around the garage out back and spun some yarn.

Soon enough, it was time for me to get back on the road. I wasn't sure which way I'd go or why. I would go wherever the wind blew, just to ride and explore.

Westbound

I had no plan once I left Jersey. I had stayed at a couple of places there and didn't want to wear my welcome out. I'm sure I could've stayed with other folks, but I'd been in Jersey for two weeks already. I never seem to get enough of being home.

I had considered driving south through Delaware on Rt. 9 as far as possible, then heading to Cape Hatteras, N.C. A ferry takes cars and trucks over to Ocracoke, N.C. It's one of my favorite spots on earth. The beaches are pristine and uninhabited.

The weather is always a concern when tent camping. The option of heading south wasn't looking good. I had well over a month before I would go home. I had time to travel.

I had been staying in touch with Dan in Scottsville. He informed me that his grass needed me to come to mow it. He generously offered to pay for the fuel for the mower. I just love Dan's sense of humor. His little chuckle at the end of some witty or slightly sarcastic comment. So, Virginia, it was.

I rolled out of Jeff's on July 27th. I took the Walt Whitman Bridge over the Delaware River and headed to Pattison Ave. in Philly. I found the football and baseball stadiums. I took pictures of my Harley out front of the Lincoln Financial Field and Citizens Bank Park, then headed south along Route 291 past the airport. I drove through Chester on Route13 and into Marcus Hook. Then I proceeded south into Delaware.

Google took me onto Darley Rd. to Rt. 3, across Northern Delaware, which is, in my estimation, beautiful. I lived in Delaware for a couple of years, from 89-91. As a teenager, I owned a 1974 Yamaha RD350. I would ride over the bridge to Delaware and get lost in the Brandywine area. There are a couple of covered bridges, as I recall, in Northern Delaware. One is Smith Bridge, which crosses the Brandywine River.

This area of the country is amazing. I once took my children on the Wilmington & Western Railroad. It was about a 2.5-hour tour with an old, coal-burning steam locomotive. In the fall, with the foliage, the ride was terrific. At different times of the year, they stage old west-style train robberies. We rented a caboose, which held the entire family. We stopped for a half-hour along White Clay Creek.

One of the most important but little-known facts about this area is the location of the Mason-Dixon Line. Most think it's much further south when the Pennsylvania/ Maryland border is that line. Even more interesting, the North/South border between Maryland and Delaware is also part of that line. There was a sliver of land between the three states, which, at one time, was a part of no state. Therefore, none had jurisdiction, and it soon became a haven for thieves and other criminals.

Once I got to Route 1, it was clear sailing, with minimal traffic. It wasn't long before I was on the open road again, getting re-centered. Now and again, I considered how nice it would be to have tunes to listen to during my journey. However, I realized that was just a distraction from getting centered. My mind would drift to home and the troubles that awaited my return.

Sometimes, fear would grip me. "What will I do if this or that happens...?"

The Bogeyman would visit me. I got plenty of practice dismissing those fears. I just focused on now and what I was seeing, feeling (physically), smelling, and hearing. It became more and more amazing with the passing miles.

There were many times I wished I had someone along with me to share all these fantastic experiences. But being by myself provided an experience I deeply needed. Being ok, being alone.

I think most of us believe we are incomplete without that special someone. I once read that "life is my soulmate." It's been there since the beginning, and it will be there at the end. Everyone else will come and go — all the crazy twists and turns we experience. Embrace it all, the love, the grief, the wonders, and the pain. It's all part of this thing we call life. Some people cannot be alone for long periods. Being alone and at peace takes practice. We inundate ourselves with stimuli constantly, and we miss some of the best parts of life. Being quiet is, for me, where I can become content.

I stopped at a McDonald's to eat. The dining room was closed, so I got my food and walked out to the bike. I sat on the ground and leaned against the front tire while picking at my fries and drinking the coke.

I had parked along the roadway, so I watched the traffic pass by. I noticed a girl who appeared to be staring in my direction from her sedan. I wondered if she was looking at me or past me. She smiled, and her hand left the steering wheel as she wiggled her fingers and smiled. I smiled and nodded as she pulled away. That moment brought to mind the lyrics of a Jackson Browne/ Glenn Fry favorite: Take it Easy. "There's a girl, my lord, in a flatbed Ford, slowin' down to have a look at me." It made my day…

It was just before dark when I arrived in. Dan and Sharon were in Jersey, so I got settled in on my own. As I laid down to sleep, a storm blew in. I had seen some storms living in Florida. I'd been caught in a couple of waterspouts/tornadoes. The weather people called this thing a microburst. Hail the size of golf balls hammered the house—wind gusting at hurricane speeds. I thought for a moment the house was coming apart.

The power went out, and I watched the lightning, so frequent and bright that you could read by it, as the hail shredded the trees and garden. A roof covered the back porch, but the deck underneath was still littered with hail and shredded leaves.

Finally, things settled down. I looked up the number for the local power company and called them. Within a couple of hours, the power was on, and I was fast asleep.

The next day, I cleaned up as much as I could before the folks got home. The damage around town was extensive. Whole trees with huge root systems turned upside-down all-around Scottsville, and branches broken from trees lay upon rooftops and cars alike. The whining sound of chainsaws filled the morning air.

I got a call from Peaches. He knew I was headed back to Virginia, and he wanted to meet for lunch in Lynchburg. He rode from Winston/Salem for about 2.5 hours. I rode for about 1.5 hours each way. It was a beautiful summer day in Virginia.

Peaches gave me a bag of his Rwandan coffee. He had just roasted it, and it smelled amazing. I couldn't wait to get back to make a cup. I gotta say, Peaches is a pretty special guy to ride five hours, just to offer a fella he met once some coffee. Y'know, I'm still amazed by the people I meet every day. There are plenty of good people that exist in each of us. We just let fear step between us and who we are.

Over lunch, we talked about Liberty University. Peaches had gone to school there years before. He told me that Liberty is one of the nation's largest non-profit universities and that they offer a wide variety of online classes today. He asked about my travels as of this trip to date. I told him of some of my fears and how I overcame them. Peaches is a bigger-than-life kind of guy, with his hearty laugh and gentle sarcasm and humor.

We hung out for a little while after lunch. Then we went our separate ways. I wanted to get back to Dan's and mow the grass. They were expected home later that day, but taking the scenic route everywhere was growing on me. I was learning to slow down a little more each day. If I could find a suitable place in that area of Virginia, I'd seriously consider moving.

I got back to the house with some daylight left. I walked out to the shed in the back, grabbed the mower, and started in. I knew I wouldn't finish the four or so acres before dark, but I wasn't in a hurry. I got down in the back behind some trees and scared up a fawn that jumped up and ran off past the tool shed. It was young enough that it still had its spots. I saw a few rabbits too.

I enjoy mowing the grass. The smell is just intoxicating for me. It tends to take me to a time when life was much simpler than the lives we live today. My Aunt Bea had a house not far from French Creek in Saegertown, PA. Her son John once took me to a dairy farm about a mile down the road, where they sold fresh milk. (I'm not sure it was even homogenized yet) They sold half-gallon glass bottles of chocolate milk, too. I have yet to find anything as rich and creamy as I remember that chocolate milk being.

The following day I rode into Charlottesville looking for sandals. My flips had flopped for the last time. The only shoes I had with me were my boots. I stopped in several thrift shops to find a bargain.

There was a garden tractor repair shop where I chose to make a U-turn to get back to one I missed. As I neared the exit, I negotiated the parking area, which sloped one way while the driveway sloped another. Plus, I needed to come to a complete stop to yield to oncoming cars.

I felt like I needed both feet on the ground, which would prevent me from using the back brake. As I grabbed the front brake, I turned the front wheel ever so slightly. That was a no-no. Gravity and momentum pulled the bike further to the left and down the slope. It was too much for me to fight, and the almost 700-pound bike went to the ground. The crash bars helped, but the bike continued to roll because of the slope. It stopped rolling when the turn signals met the ground, and I hopped off into the road.

I caught my balance and looked the bike over for damage. I backed up to it, grabbed the back fender and handlebar, and with a great heave, pulled it up until I could put the kickstand down. The turn signals were scratched slightly, as were the crash bars, but there was no visible damage. Being scared by the mishap, I got the hell out of there, only to realize after a few miles that my lens cover on the rear left signal was gone. I turned back and found it, in one piece, no less. I put it back on, and I was on my way again.

I think the things that run through my head when that kind of thing happens may be typical. The bike was "cherry" before, just a few minutes ago. Now, it was "damaged goods." I had entertained thoughts of selling the bike once I returned home, thinking I might even get more than I paid for it, but now "no one would want it, looking like this."

As I rode back to the house, I felt the bike out. It wasn't off. It felt great. But I was still upset with myself for having dropped it. It could've been avoided. I thought it over and decided, "It's now all mine. It's got my mark on it." Acceptance would provide peace of mind. That didn't mean I had to like it; it just meant it is what it is.

Dan and Sharon took off for a few days and left me in charge. Of what I'm not certain, but I took care of the family dog, or the dog took care of me, one or the other. Their daughter Danielle and her family lived nearby. I picked tomatoes for them. They were ripening while I was picking them. I couldn't seem to keep up. The little cherry tomatoes were delicious. I stood by the plants and just picked and ate them while they were still warm from the summer sun.

When Sharon and Dan returned, we took a bike ride together. Dan and I swapped bikes for a while. His Yamaha handled entirely differently than my Harley. The anti-lock braking system was much better. But I got a chance to see my baby from a different perspective. I chose the "Soft Tail Slim" because of the seat height. At 23", I believe it's the lowest available. I'm 5'-6" and shrinking.

It's called a "Slim" because of its appearance from the rear. I love the look of this bike from the factory with its sleek Bobber design, low profile, and fat tires. Putting a windshield, the passenger seat, and the sissy bar on this handsome machine detract from its profile considerably. Even so, it still commands lots of attention. Following Dan through the countryside and watching him lean around corners gave me a new appreciation. I know just how good this baby looks.

I left Scottsville Friday, August 6, by way of Route 20. On the way, I found and fell in love with Plank Road. It winds through the countryside, covered by trees in places, making it cool and shady. The hills were subtle, but I could feel the temperature changes as I moved from the shade to the sunlight and back.

Rolling farmland sprawled across the countryside, disappearing into the mountains in the distance. It was one of those roads you wished went on forever.

I rode through the Port Republic and later took a detour into Lost River State Park in Mathias, WV. I stopped to get a few pictures of the park, which beautifully landscaped. I looked for the "Lost River," but I couldn't find it. I guess that's why they call it "Lost River."

I would have loved to stay and do a little more investigation there, but my lollygagging had already taken quite a bit of time. Rather than backtracking, I continued through Route 12. Although the road was somewhat rough, the scenery was breathtaking.

I stopped to take photos at a bend in the road. With the barbed wire fence, I'm certain this is exactly what this place looked like 100 or even 200 years ago. A bicyclist stopped, and we chatted for a while. I think I was more amazed at his journey than he was at mine, pedaling a bicycle over thirty miles one way with a backpack, up and down hills, over roads that leave much to be desired, even with good suspension. I could only imagine how beautiful this area was in the fall and winter.

I passed through Deep Creek, a beautiful lake in the mountains. There were boaters everywhere. Even just passing by, I was sure this was a summer paradise. I drove around a little, looking for overnight accommodations and taking in the sights. It seemed like it would be fairly expensive to book a hotel or an Airbnb. I had to keep moving.

I continued on Garrett Highway to Friendsville Road, Main Street, National Pike, and finally to Uniontown, PA. Uniontown is a quaint old city founded on July 4th,1776. It is also known for its role in the coal and steel industry, and there was a bloody labor battle in 1894. On a happier note, in 1967, the Big Mac was born there.

I stopped and searched for a place to land for the night. A campground, Airbnb, or cheap motel would do at that point. I found an Airbnb in Rockwood, an hour east. I typically don't like backtracking. However, Airbnb doesn't give you the exact address until you book. In this case, I didn't mind so much, because the scenery was so beautiful. I traveled through Connellsville, east on Sculliton Road. As I was crossing Laurel Hill Creek, I stumbled onto a covered bridge. Kings Bridge, erected in 1802, was rebuilt in 1906 and 2008. Driving across isn't permitted, but the photo ops are plentiful here.

I had booked a bed in a hostel. I'm not certain what the place at 506 Main Street was before, but I suspect it had been a restaurant at one time. There was a door from an old walk-in freezer and a pass-thru window from the inside of the cooler to the supposed serving area. There was a railroad less than 100 yards behind the place.

Inside there were possibly a dozen sets of bunk beds to accommodate travelers. Of the fellas that bunked in, one was from Mexico. He was working nearby. Four more were cyclists traveling from Pittsburgh to West Virginia on a three or four-day tour. They told me of old railroad beds that are bike paths and bragged about the scenery there. They all lived in West Virginia and worked together. They had someone haul them and their bikes to Pittsburgh, drop them off, and ride home.

At 5:00 am, a train rolled by. I could hear its whistle coming a mile or more away. I went out back to greet it with my camera. As I watched the rail cars roll past, I wondered about each car's history, where they had been, and what they had seen. Hobos had probably ridden these rails a century ago.

I packed up the bike and headed out to find coffee. My thoughts turned to the guy from Mexico. We had shared intimate details of our lives concerning our families. I spoke of how I had traveled for work when I was his age and the havoc it and drinking had created in my marriage and family life. Being an absent father wasn't good for any of us. He was well aware of the dangers and promised to get settled in his home in North Carolina. I still think of that fella from time to time.

I found a small shopping center called Highlands Market on County Line Road in Champion, Pa. I stopped in as they were opening. I needed to get coffee. There were little tables out front, where I sat and drank my coffee. At its best, this area seems like it might be "Suburban Life"—larger properties with beautiful homes and a manicured golf course. The cars that pulled in and out shouted money.

One fella with an apparent hangover stepped from his SUV. He gave me the notion that my life was pretty good. I just needed to keep things simple. A couple of guys sat at the table adjacent to me. They asked the same questions. Some of the answers I provided varied, but if someone asked, "Hello! How are you?"

My reply was typical, "Pretty good for an 'ol' fat guy."

DAVID RICKERSON Sr.

It made for a laugh and opened the door for a bit of conversation.

If they asked where I came from, my answer was "Florida."

But should they ask where I was headed, and most did, my answer was simple. "I'm not sure."

The truth is, we don't know. I may have a plan, but life happens. I try to school myself into thinking every day is an adventure. I never know what's around the next corner.

I finished my coffee and headed off into the rest of this adventure.

I had no idea I would pass through Pittsburgh again until I saw one of the bridges. Those old iron bridges were pretty easy to identify. I stopped and called my cousin Tera. I didn't want to be that close and not reach out. She invited me to come by for a visit, but I insisted I must move on. I had contacted my buddy Mike in Ohio. I was going to see him and his family earlier in the trip, but the weather didn't permit it. Now the weather looked fine for the next few days.

After another hour or so of riding, I began to get tired. I came upon an old cemetery along the road with plenty of shade trees. I pulled in and found the perfect spot to park the Harley and catch a few winks. As I was dozing off, it dawned on me that I was going through Ohio, and Dr. Robert Smith's house is in Akron. I should stop in and take a tour.

Dr. Bob was the co-founder of A.A. His home is a historical site that we folks in the recovery world cherish. I found my way to Akron and pulled up across the street from the house. I parked the bike and crossed the road. As I climbed the front steps, I heard, "Welcome home."

I looked up to see a volunteer standing on the front porch waiting for me. A friend of mine once visited there. Ed was met with the same words when he pardoned himself, stating he had his small dog with him. The volunteer replied, "It's as much your home as anyone's."

That happened several years ago. I think the policies are different these days. But all in all, it was pretty difficult not to feel welcome there.

It was 2:15, and the sign on the door had the open hours posted from 11:00 am to 3:00 pm. Today was Saturday. I was told to take my time walking through. I was given a private tour, from the coffee pot in the kitchen to the attic. But down in the basement, I was on my own.

There were two other visitors whose accents I recognized immediately. They were from Cinnaminson, New Jersey. We had coffee together at the kitchen table, and we talked like old friends. We sat on the front porch for over an hour when the house closed.

Val and Helen had sold their home in Jersey. They purchased a new Chevrolet cargo van, put a mattress in the back, a luggage compartment on the roof, and took off to see America like a couple of old Hippies. They were on their way back from the west coast. (Side note: As of this writing, they are still on the road, headed to Baja for the winter.)

People came up to the porch, which was outfitted with plenty of seating. We greeted those folks with "Welcome home," just as we had been greeted. Those who came sat with us and chatted like old friends.

Helen asked me where I was staying. I replied that I hadn't decided yet whether I would camp or find an

Airbnb. They said, "We're camping, and we have room at the campsite. Please come stay with us."

I'm the kinda guy that gets a little weird when I'm offered things like this. However, I had no problem inviting other people to do the same things. I was non-committal, but I thanked them and said I would think it over.

We considered getting dinner together. Helen and Val looked at a few local menus, but I had my heart set on pizza. We exchanged numbers, and finally, I rolled out to find some pie.

As I traveled around Akron, I decided to drive past The Seiberling Estate. At the historic gatehouse was where Dr. Bob agreed to meet Bill Wilson for "15 minutes, no more."

The two men remained there, talking for almost six hours. That was the beginning of something that would go on to change and save millions of lives worldwide. The story is incredibly interesting and can be read in the book titled Alcoholics Anonymous.

At some point, I realized I was very close to Kent State University. I decided to ride there and see if there was some type of a memorial for the students who were murdered there in May 1970 by the National Guard. To this end, Google can be extremely helpful with many of my travel needs. I found the site, parked the bike, and wandered around. Several other folks walked around the campus, looking at the memorials. I began to take photos.

There were four memorials, one for each student that died. Each one was in a parking space with six columns that I believe are lit in the evenings. The top of each column had a granite cap. People had placed stones and other trinkets atop these.

In one corner of the space was a triangular granite slab with the date May 4, 1970, and the student's name. There were also other markers placed where other students were shot but survived.

I remember well that fateful day when those trusted to uphold the Constitution fired on a group of students protesting the Vietnam war. Students began throwing rocks at the guardsmen. In fear for their lives, the guardsmen opened fire on the unarmed students.

I found the metal sculpture with a single bullet hole through it. I raised my phone to the hole, and in video mode, I recorded with the camera lens, looking through the hole toward the parking area, where the four students had lain, dying. As I spoke about what I was filming, I backed the camera away to see the bullet hole and the sculpture with the markers in the parking area. I still find it terribly disturbing that something like this happened in America.

This is now considered a National Historic Site. There's a museum, but it was closed Saturday afternoon. I left the University campus pretty somber and headed back to Akron. I thought, *Why didn't you just say yes to the offer of camping with them? What could it hurt to walk through a door that the universe has opened*?

I called Helen, got the address, and headed toward the campground when it began to rain. Looking for a spot to stay dry, I spotted a drive-thru bank. There were several bays, two of which had ATMs, so I chose one of the others.

When the bike was packed, I could lean against the pack and nod off with my feet over the crash bars. It was similar to a recliner. I hadn't even fallen off as of yet.

Once under the overhang, I put my phone in the Ram Phone mount and lay back to watch the Phillies game on my phone while my travels were in a rain delay.

The game finished just as the rain let up, and I headed to the campground. It was nearing dark. It took just a few minutes to put my tent up, and we sat at the picnic table. Bug spray was useless against the mosquitoes that were probably a quarter pound each. With coordinated efforts, they could've picked up the tent with my fat ass in it and flown me off to a smorgasbord, so I got into the van's passenger seat, with Val and Helen in the back. We told story after story. I doubt any of us had laughed this hard in quite a while. We drunks have some pretty funny stories. Well, at least the parts we remember.

It got late, and finally, we said goodnight.

The next morning, we rose early. I packed up between mosquito attacks, and we were off to find coffee. They had asked me to join them at an AA breakfast; I agreed this time. I believe it was at Guy's Party Center. There were over 100 people who joined us, the food was way more than adequate, the price was very reasonable, and to top it off, the Home Group members would not let us pay. We tipped well. As we were leaving, we decided to visit Dr. Bob's grave. It just happened to be Dr. Bob's birthday, so we bought a cake and took it back to Dr. Bob's house and shared it with other visitors and volunteers.

I got off easy because I went back to the house to clear a path for the cake while they drove from store to store to find one. Finally, the cake arrived. We were instructed to cut it in the back house and put out plates and napkins. After having coffee again, the three of us retired to the front porch.

I made my way to the gift shop next door and purchased a single bronze medallion with the inscription "Dr. Bob's Home." I planned on attending more meetings along the way. The thought came to me that I could pull that medallion from my pocket each time at the end of the meeting. I would explain where I had gotten it and that it was for my sponsor. I'd pass it around the room and ask people to say a blessing for my sponsor and his family. Like people everywhere, they were going through a rough time.

After closing Dr. Bob's, we left and got a bite to eat and said our goodbyes with hugs and love. Then I headed off toward Gibsonburg, Ohio.

Ohio is mostly rural but pretty flat. The towns I passed through were much like those I'd seen in Pennsylvania and New York. I pulled into Mike's about dusk. His wife, Julie, was out in her Corvette with a cousin. Mike showed me around the house. They added it to the garage a few years ago. Here was the Man Cave. The centerpiece was a pool table, and there were beer signs of all sorts hung from every wall and the sloped ceiling. Mike and I honed our skills as teenagers at the family-owned bar in Penns Grove; The R&R. Here stood the R&R West. Deb, who is a part of the story and mentioned earlier in this writing, worked there for some time.

Mike and I, as kids, were pretty typical. Well, maybe not so much. We were the kids who thought every night was mischief night. Mike had a tree fort behind his house, and that was where we practiced kissing girls and smoking cigarettes and Marijuana. Somehow, Mike was always the one that got caught. I, on the other hand, always seemed to get away.

One time, Mike and I were walking along Main Street in front of the A&P. Just in front of us was an old lady. I hurriedly approached from behind her and gave her a boot in the rear end. Not hard, just enough to get her attention. As she turned around, I continued around behind her. She grabbed Michael and started shaking him. Of course, I was gone, and she never saw me. I guess maybe I was the original jackass.

Mike and I once lit a bag of dog poop on fire on Mr. W's front porch. We knocked on the door and ran. I ducked behind the bushes across the street. Mike ran down the entire driveway through the backyard. When Mr. W came to the door, he saw Mike, yelled out his last name, and then gave chase. Mr. W. ran right past me, hiding in the bushes. I got away. Mike didn't. I'd like to tell you which of us was the mastermind of that caper, but we swore to secrecy many years ago.

As Mike took me through the house, I saw some tile work that needed to be addressed. I promised him I would fix that. We picked up what we needed the next day, and I made the small repair.

The following day they took me around town, actually a couple of towns. Because it was Monday, most of the shops were not open. We drove to a park along Lake Erie. We walked along the shore and took photographs.

Mike is a great photographer. He's got a keen eye for interesting subjects. My buddy Dan does, as well. When I'm looking for a shot, I'm looking for something that will provoke emotion, whether it's in a still life or someone's smile. The best pictures aren't people posing for the camera. It's candid shots of people being people.

My personal favorites are laughing, eating, and staring off into space with a sullen look.

I knew it was still about 1,200 miles to Sturgis, SD. At a couple of hundred miles a day, I could get there by Saturday, the last day of bike week. A couple of hundred miles was all the further I wanted to ride in a day if I could. There's always some backtracking and missed turns, let alone the probability of driving out of the way to get an Airbnb.

Watching the weather closely, I thought it best to cut my stay to two nights with Mike and Julie. Their daughter Lexi came by to say hello. She's such a great woman; beautiful, intelligent, modest, and nice. They'd done a great job with her.

I put 270 miles behind me getting to just beyond Joliet, Illinois. There was an Airbnb that was reasonable there. Marshall was the owner, a well-educated woman who worked for the Department of Homeland Security. We chatted for a bit before I turned in. I wasn't interested in dinner so much as I was getting sleep. Typically, when I entered a new place, I looked around and found things that needed to be fixed —here was no different. The seat on the commode was loose, so I took the liberty of tightening it for her.

The next morning, I found myself on the road early, looking for coffee. I cannot ride a motorcycle and drink coffee at the same time, so I typically sat on a curb outside of a gas station and had a cup. The sky was blue, and the road was straight. There was not much to look at other than grain silos and corn as far as one could see. At that point, I decided to fill up when I reached a half tank.

Taking back roads provided me with plenty of time with the road all to myself. The sky ahead looked kind of a funny color blue. It appeared as though it might rain. I pulled over to get my slicker on once again. At least I could take my time. In just a few minutes, I was back on the road again.

It wasn't long before the weather turned bad. I approached an intersection and saw an electric company truck coming to a stop. I had the yellow blinking light and the right of way. He didn't see me and began to pull out before coming to a complete stop. He was in a hurry, which indicated that bad, bad weather might be on the way. I progressively applied my brakes. The bike skidded a little sideways, but the riding course prepared me for just this scenario. My eyes were on him, and I expected him to pull out. I got around him and continued on my way.

I had been through some bad weather; the storm at Danny's, the storm with Kim and we get terrible storms in Florida.

My daughter and I were camping once at Ft. Desoto in late April, ten or eleven years ago, when a waterspout came ashore at midnight and destroyed our campsite and a few alongside us. She and I, along with the tent, were thrown into a tree. That twister broke two

113

large trees, one within ten feet of us, the other thirty feet away. My friend Ronnie was there for that, too.

The following year, at a customer's house on Indian Shores, they informed me that a large waterspout was twelve miles offshore, "but we'll be safe," (famous last words). We narrowly escaped as it jumped over their beachfront cottage and took down an Australian pine about 50 ft. high, just missing my van and his car.

That tornado continued through Pinellas County, flipping cars over along Ulmerton Road. So, I tend to get somewhat nervous when I see a storm coming, especially when I have no shelter. I was in the middle of nowhere, with nothing but corn in every direction. My 700lb bike was blown around like it was a sheet of plywood in a windstorm, even when I slowed to 20 mph. So, I stopped and put the kickstand down.

The wind and rain were so fierce that I thought the bike would blow over. I stood beside it and held onto it for all I was worth. It rocked back and forth in the gales. I kept looking for a tornado, but there was nowhere to run or hide even if I saw one. After a solid half-hour, it began to slow down. I waited until the rain almost stopped, composed myself as best I could, and forged ahead.

I was about four miles from Mendota on Walter Payton Memorial Highway when I had to stop. There were power lines down across the road. A gentleman sent me to a side street, but power lines were also down there.

The homeowners told me to cut through their yard, which I did, but riding a 700-pound bike through someone's lawn when it was saturated was interesting. Trees were down everywhere, branches on cars and houses; the damage to some places was extensive. Casey's gas station was the only place that had auxiliary power. I fueled up and got underway, going west again.

West of the Mississippi

I crossed the Mississippi into Clinton, Iowa. I had considered getting an oil change at the Harley dealership because I knew I only had a thousand miles to go, so I stopped by to get a price. While they didn't hold a gun to my head, asking me for that kind of money for 3 quarts of oil and a filter, it still felt like highway robbery, so I decided to take a pass. I did, however, buy a poker chip from them and looked over their inventory. They had a beautiful red and white Indian Chieftain.

I believe it was Wheatland, Iowa, where I found an old 1960 pink Rambler Ambassador parked in someone's yard. It was decorated with mannequins climbing in at least three of the windows. There was an Elvis statue leaning against the front of the house, playing guitar, with a half dozen Elvis heads planted along the street. There were just as many vinyl records. I had to go back and take some photos.

One of my favorite attractions to taking back roads was things that you could run across if you're paying attention. So many times, I'd drive along, and my passenger was buried in their phone. Why travel hundreds or thousands of miles to only catch glimpses of a small part of the trip? Why not just download Google Earth on the phone, stay home, out of traffic and kill two birds with one stone? Look at the money that would be saved on hotels and gas. Even with all the scenic stops, and time to take photos, I made it to Cedar Rapids, Iowa, that afternoon.

I packed the bike up and headed for my morning coffee the following day. While I sat on the curb drinking the brew, I found an AA meeting in the Meeting Guide App. It was a clubhouse, and usually, those places follow through with scheduled meetings, as was the case here, so I made my way there.

A woman showed me around the place, and we talked for a half-hour or so. She suggested I move my bike before the shop opened next door. "It'll get towed," she said.

I moved the bike around the corner and went back upstairs. I enjoy attending meetings away from home.

The people are always congenial, and it was no different here.

I was planning to put a little over 250 miles in today. I rode around town a little, looking for a mom-and-pop restaurant. I stopped at St. Andrew's Grill and Bar in State Center, Iowa. The burger was good, but the service was slow. But in some places, life is a bit slower. The town itself was pretty cool.

I set out for a Walmart and found one in Fort Dodge. It was a few miles out of the way, but I needed a few items that I didn't have up to this point, specifically Chapstick and sunblock. I was getting cooked in the Midwest sun.

I did just a bit of sightseeing around Fort Dodge before getting back to the road.

An hour or so later, I needed fuel and spotted a station in Holstein, Iowa. As I was pumping gas, I looked over at this quaint village and thought, *Let's go take a look. It's so cute!*

I crossed the road and passed a sign in English and German welcoming me to Holstein. All the homes were nice, and the lawns were manicured. It reminded me of an old Monkees song, "Pleasant Valley Sunday," as I drove up and down their streets. I just had to sing that song.

I had passed a little league baseball field on my way in town and circled to inspect it closer. I hoped to find a picnic table to nap on. The weather was clear, and it was hot in the sun, but it would be perfect napping weather in the shade. No picnic table, the tree-lined street would have to be sufficient. I parked beneath a beautiful shade tree, cocked the front wheel, and assumed the position. My butt was sore, and my eyes were tired. In a moment, I was fast asleep.

I heard a vehicle slow down and back up and was uncertain how much time had passed. A creaky door opened, and a man's voice called out, "Hey, are you ok over there? Is everything alright?"

Without moving from my napping position or even turning my head, I replied, "Man, I haven't got a care in the world."

I stood up slowly to see him a little better, and he crossed the street with a big ole bushy-bearded smile and his hand out. I introduced myself and looked over at his old truck. Then I noticed his garage. It was three bays, a

DAVID RICKERSON Sr.

nice-sized workshop —something I'd love to have. "Man, that's one beautiful garage," I said to Dan.

He replied, "That right, there ain't no garage. That's whatcha call a marriage saver right there!"

I laughed and nodded. I had to see it, and he invited me over, so we walked across the street to take a closer look. He asked where I was traveling from and said he suspected I was headed to Sturgis.

In that "marriage saver," he had some four-wheelers, a few tools, and a '69 Mustang. It was his first car. It looked well cared for, but it had a sunroof, and I commented that I didn't know they had those. He informed me that it was the mistake of a seventeen-year-old, and we laughed. We traded a few stories about cars we'd owned and wished we still did.

I noticed a big camper in his yard and asked if he knew of any nearby campgrounds. I was thinking that maybe I was done riding for the day. It was about 5 pm, and while I still had plenty of daylight left, I was ready to start looking.

He thought for a moment and asked if I was "OK to camp alone or if I needed to be around other folks."

I wasn't quite sure why he asked that, but I answered, "Oh, I'm fine either way."

He continued, "Well, my wife and myself are on the board for the county fair, and I have keys to the property. It's about eleven miles out of town. It's really pretty out there, and you'll have the whole place to yourself if ya wanna do that. I'll open the bathrooms, so you'll have a shower and all that stuff."

I needed to get food in me, so I went back to the gas station and got some chicken. I got a couple of bottles of Gatorade as well and rode back over to his house.

He introduced me to his wife, Peg, and I followed them out of town. It was an hour or so before dusk when we got there. He made certain I was all settled in before they left me. They were going somewhere early the next morning, so we said our goodbyes and traded phone numbers. We have been in touch ever since. He calls now and then, or I'll call him, and I've invited them to come to Florida when they're tired of the snow.

I got my tent set up and walked around the fairgrounds. There was a fenced-off area for a Rodeo and paddocks for the horses, along with a covered arena and plenty of other things to inspect while I was there. Surrounding the fairgrounds were beautiful rolling hills with giant wind turbine generators. I saw those for the last couple of days, but here was a chance to watch them operate.

I took pictures as the sun set. It was so peaceful there. I was at least a couple hundred yards from a road, were very few cars passed.

As the night came, so did the stars. There were a few clouds, but still an amazing view. I didn't have a chair with me, so I lay on the picnic table with a pillow beneath my head, looking up, completely grateful for everything I had.

At first light, I broke camp. I headed back to the same gas station but stopped by the couple's house first to thank them. They were getting ready to roll out. I let them know I picked up what little trash I had found on the ground so that I left it better than I found it. They were both appreciative, as was I.

I got coffee at the station, and a motorcycle pulled in to fuel up. The couple got off and told me they were headed back to Pennsylvania from Sturgis. He worked at a Harley dealership. We traded numbers. It is incredible how motorcycle people just seem to connect. I finished my coffee and headed out.

Soon, I crossed into Nebraska. There, I found Granny's Restaurant. Just what I was looking for, some home cooking. I'd been riding for days, and I had seen hundreds of chicken farms but no place to cook all those eggs. Many of the old-fashioned places were closed. This one was not, but I could tell they couldn't get help.

I grabbed a table and ordered coffee. Typically, I would order two eggs over easy, potatoes, toast, and bacon. The eggs were free-range and looked great. I watched the woman slice the loaves of bread in the back. "Granny's" got two thumbs up from me!

Once I got back on the bike, I noticed a change in the topography. The further into Nebraska I rode, the prettier it got. I was completely blown away by the beauty of the rolling hills. Had someone asked me early that morning what I might think of Nebraska, I would never have guessed it would be like this. I would certainly consider this a place to live if it weren't for the snow. I stopped and turned back to take photos of valleys, long dirt roads, and anything else that caught my interest; there sure was plenty of that.

I continued on the Outlaw Trail Scenic Byway to Crofton, Nebraska. I'd seen a sign that indicated some kind of landmark there for Lewis and Clark. I turned where it said, but I rode up and down the streets and found nothing.

I was thirsty, so I dropped into the Lewis & Clark Mini Mart, where I bought a bottle of water and a snack. While outside next to my bike, a young, extremely attractive woman approached from her vehicle. She offered a "hello" on her way into the mart.

I was sitting on a bench, and she stopped and asked where I was from. We struck up a conversation about the beauty of this part of Nebraska and several other things.

Nicolette introduced herself and told me she was an avid hunter, and her son had gotten his first deer last year. She was very proud of her son. I told Nicholette I thought the town was quaint. I had ridden up and down several of the streets looking for the Lewis & Clark Museum, which I had seen advertised on a sign, and asked her if there were anything I should see while I was there. She suggested I check out the Lewis and Clark Dam and Museum, ten or eleven miles away.

She spent most of her lunch hour chatting with me. It's not often you find folks to be that congenial. Maybe it is me, but people can be rude. I'll open the door for somebody, and they'll act as if they did me some kind of a favor. No "thank you," nothing. Too many people have too little respect for others or Mother Earth and have a sense of entitlement. Their parents failed to teach them manners. People like Nicholette are refreshing. I like friendly people. If you're not friendly, change it. It's your responsibility.

After she finished her lunch, I left and rode out to find the dam. The roads were smooth and scenic. I assumed I might have to come back this way, not knowing where I was and what roads go where, but I was learning to trust Google more and more.

As I pulled into the parking area, there was a bus full of children. I'm going to assume it was probably vacation bible school. In mid-August, schools would still be out.

I took the Nikon out of the saddlebag and walked to the overlook. The view was nice but seemed like it was lacking something. Nicholette had said there was much more to see if I crossed the dam. So after a few moments, I rode toward the dam. I wanted to get off and take pictures on the top of the dam, but there wasn't a stopping area, so I proceeded to the other side of the Missouri River. There were several folks fishing. Again,

I got the Nikon out and started shooting. In fact, the Lewis and Clark Dam, that whole area was beautiful.

As I crossed the dam, I also crossed into South Dakota. Back on the road, I would continue along for 320 miles for the day.

I stopped at Lynn's Dakotamart for some food. I spotted a Tribal cop —I was on a Crow Reservation. I approached him for information about a possible camping facility nearby. He suggested a weekend sweat, something I would have loved to do, but it was Friday. I had one more day to make the end of Sturgis, so I had to decline the opportunity.

The campground was right around the bend. I pulled into the "Left Tailrace Office." The gentleman I spoke with had been to Sturgis dozens of times. He made some recommendations for lodging the next night and hooked me up with a good spot for this night. He encouraged me to purchase the national park pass, and I did.

It was dusk when I set my tent up. Boaters were coming back to the ramp after the day of fun on the wide Missouri at Crow Creek Reservation. As the sky darkened, I thought, we're due for the Perseids meteor showers.

The peak was the night before, while I was in Iowa. I guessed I'd fallen asleep too early, but I might see a few tonight. I've learned how to use my Samsung Galaxy Note 10 in Pro mode. With the proper adjustment and using the S pen to operate the shutter, pictures of stars are quite simple. The ambient light wasn't too intrusive. Needless to say, I didn't get much sleep.

I tried to be smart about my fuel. When I got down to approximately a half tank, I had already begun to look for a place to stop. I was getting about 46MPG, and the bike has a five-gallon tank. The Harley uses premium fuel, so it's a little pricey.

I stopped at McDonald's in Pierre, SD, and had a bite to eat. I crossed the bridge over the Missouri river and decided I needed to get fuel. I didn't trust that I'd find another station anytime soon, so I backtracked over the bridge and found a gas station. Most of the stations I encountered only carried fuel with 91 octane and below. After refueling at a place that sold fuel for farm equipment (diesel is cheaper for them, no road taxes) and losing a little time backtracking, I felt the need to hurry, so I did. A minute or so along, I saw lights behind me and heard a siren.

This would be my second ticket on this journey. The first was a red-light ticket from a camera in Delaware. I rolled through the red light on a right-hand turn. The officer asked if I knew why he had pulled me over.

I wanted to say, "Uh. Because I don't have a seat belt on?" But I was obviously speeding.

He was kind enough to give me a reduced speeding ticket. For a moment, I considered fighting it. After all, he lied on the ticket about my actual speed. His credibility was questionable, right? Instead, I thought, "Don't let it ruin the day."

It was Saturday morning, and I wanted to make Sturgis.

I passed huge fields of sunflowers that seemed to go on forever. I pulled off a couple of times, looking for the right shot, but couldn't find it. I wrapped the Nikon in a microfiber hand towel and wedged it between the windscreen and the handlebars. I pulled on it, and it seemed safe.

There were a couple of old abandoned houses that would make for great photos, so I stopped and took a few pictures. I saw a couple of bikes coming toward me from the west, so I pulled the camera up and began to shoot. As they passed, I returned the Nikon to its nest and pulled away quickly as a couple of bikes came from behind. I got fifty yards down the road and the camera launched from its nest to the ground, breaking the lens off the camera.

I slowed and turned back to pick up the pieces. Nothing worked. The Nikon was finished. The emotions I suddenly experienced washed over me like floodwater; I should've never come. Carrying my camera that way was a bad idea. I should just turn around and go home.

As with the ticket I had just gotten, I told myself this was OK. The committee in my head didn't agree but said, "Ok, we won't let it ruin our day."

Riding further west, I saw a sign that said I would need to turn to get to the Badlands. I wanted to see the Badlands but passed it up. I was already running later than I wanted.

Once I arrived at Sturgis, I stopped in one of the big camping spots. I parked the bike, walked up to the office window, and asked about camping. They wanted $150.00 for two nights. Most of the entertainment was finished, and they no longer ran the shuttles into town, so I figured I'd find another spot that I had called earlier that had room. They wanted $25.00 a night.

I rode up and down a few streets until I spotted a sign for camping and stopped. The woman told me it'd be $20.00 a night. I paid her and pitched my tent in the backyard along with a few others. One fella camping there had stayed here every year for some time. He was kind of the bouncer, and he let me know who was in charge. I finished up and walked uptown.

I was just a few blocks away from an AA/NA clubhouse. There was a meeting coming up pretty soon, so I stopped and bought a couple of bottles of water from a vendor and walked up to the clubhouse. There were several people waiting, but no one showed up with a key, so we sat and talked and watched the topless girls riding by.

A young fella I sat alongside was from northern Minnesota. We struck up a conversation, and he asked where I was from. I explained that I was from Florida.

He asked if I had ridden out to Sturgis. I explained the whole trip to him and that I had ridden all back roads except for one part of my trip in New Jersey. I continued to tell him about the stretch of I-295 I traveled, going to an AA meeting in Penns Grove, N.J.

He stopped me and said he "had just finished a job in Penns Grove."

Knowing he was mistaken, I shook my head and said, "I doubt that. There's really not much there. The whole town is pretty much boarded up."

He said, "No, I'm telling you that was it! And there's another town next to it." He thought while I insisted, he'd gotten the name wrong, then he shouted, "Carneys Point."

I was dumbfounded. He was there! What are the chances? It's a little Podunk town no one has ever heard of.

Finally, someone came with a key, and we filtered inside into the airconditioned place. I sat next to my new friend while the meeting took shape. They usually ask if there were any out-of-town visitors (almost everyone). A guy across the room raised his hand, and it went around to his left. Then a fella stated, "My name is Louis, and I'm an addict from St. Pete, Florida."

I jumped to my feet and hollered, "Louis! Are you following me? Did my wife send you out to track me down?"

He hollered back, "Dave, what the hell are you doing here?"

I've known Louis for well over twenty years. Again, I asked, what were the chances?

We hung out after the meeting. We got some chow, then ice cream, and we walked around, people watching.

Later that night, after Louis and I said goodbye, I headed home to my tent. I stopped to help a couple with a selfie they were trying to take. I asked them where they were from, and he announced, "from Idaho."

Then he asked me where I was from, and I told him St Pete, Fl.

He replied, "Oh, my dad lives near there. Have you ever heard of Gulfport?"

I just looked at this guy in amazement. I shook my head. I said, "I actually live in Gulfport. I just didn't think you'd know where that was."

I asked where his pop lived in Gulfport, and it turned out he was three blocks from my house. When I asked if his old man had an old, white box truck, he was in disbelief. I once helped him get his big ole box truck home when it broke down.

Three times in a few hours. That was just too weird. I guess the Universe was just letting me know that I was right where I was supposed to be.

I returned to my tent for the night, and as I lay listening to the nearby stage broadcasting what some people call entertainment, I took some time and poured over the last few weeks. How centered I had gotten. The things that would typically put me into a tailspin didn't. They weren't bothering me whatsoever. I thought about riding across South Dakota and how the smell of sage filled the air. I thought about the baseball field I found earlier in the day that gave me a place to rest on a picnic table, in the shade, in some other little village in South Dakota.

I thought back to my second day on the road when I was heading to Asheville and how I decided that riding a motorcycle was, without a doubt, the best way to see rural America. Then, I realized how wrong I was. 125 years ago, horse and buggy would have been an even better means of travel. It was slower, and you didn't have to watch the road. The horse took care of that. The driver was free to enjoy the scenery or take a nap.

At some point, I remembered that as a child, and probably most of my adult life, I wished I could've been a cowboy, roaming the wild west on horseback and camping out under the desert sky, with no particular place to go and no set time to get there. Then, I figured this is probably as close as I might ever get or need to be.

Y'know, I'm like most folk. I spent most of my life chasing happiness. I've chased it in and out of relationships, jobs, prestige, power, bottles, gamblin'; you name it. If I thought it was gonna make me happy, I chased it. The funny thing about happiness is that it seems like it's always "over there."

Here's the secret…

Happiness isn't in having what I want; it's in wanting what I already have. It's about appreciating my life as it is at this moment. You see, the only place I never looked for happiness was the one place I thought I wouldn't find it, right under my feet. Right Here. Right Now.

The lie I think we all tell ourselves is, "I'll be alright."

"I'll be ok when the check comes," or "I'll be ok when I go on vacation."

We tell ourselves that "being ok" is over there, somewhere.

Fact is, I believe we're right where we're supposed to be at this moment. It may not feel like it, nor look like it, especially when things are going awry. It took some time and honesty to realize that the crummy stuff in life has given me my greatest lessons. There's no greater loss than losing a child, but even that has given me purpose.

A few years ago, I began a project to help families and friends who have lost someone to drug addiction or alcoholism to heal. You'll find a link later in this book. You may know someone like that who would benefit from the website. Feel free to check it out.

Sunday morning, I found myself at Uncle Louie's for breakfast. I was instructed to find the Spearfish Canyon and Needles by several folks there. I wasn't quite sure what I was looking for, but how lost could I get? I didn't bring my pack because I planned on heading back to Sturgis that afternoon.

I drove past Deadwood thru Spearfish Canyon. I stopped at several places to take photos and videos with my phone. I saw a sign for The Devil's Bathtub. I pulled into the parking area and thought, This'll be great! (I'm so stupid sometimes)

I walked and noticed a couple of young ladies just in front of me. One carried a small dog. It jumped from her arms and hit the ground with a thud.

I said, "Oh, that's terrible! Why did you throw your little dog on the ground? That wasn't nice at all!"

Her girlfriend started to giggle, and I made a couple more slightly sarcastic comments. We laughed pretty good. I then asked if we could walk together if she promised not to throw me on the ground too. We laughed a little more and continued walking. None of us had any idea how far we would need to walk.

It was 90°. I was wearing bike boots, jeans, and a black shirt, not exactly hiking clothes.

We crossed a stream several times, back and forth. The rocks had moss on them and were slippery. My smooth-soled boots made this very interesting. I caught myself a couple of times, almost going down for the count. We walked for a half-hour.

Now I'm 65 years old, and the furthest I typically walked was back from the bathroom (at 65, you're usually running to get there). I have neuropathy in both feet means the front half of my feet is numb and tingly, which translates to poor balance, even on flat ground. I was soaking wet from sweat and was at the point of turning around, but I figured we gotta be almost there. Keep going, Dave, I'd tell myself.

About ten minutes later, a family appeared, coming in the opposite direction, and I asked, "How much further?"

The woman replied, "Oh, another twenty or thirty minutes."

At that news, I shouted, "Hey, thanks, girls, for the company, but I'm going back with these folks. I'm gonna look this shit up on YouTube from the safety of my sofa."

I really didn't have that kind of time to invest that day. There was more I wanted to see. Back on the bike,

I crossed Pactola Lake Reservoir. The overlook was amazing. These lakes, surrounded by mountains, looked so tranquil.

I stopped at places along the way to take photos and found babbling brooks with wildflowers growing alongside them and the jagged rock walls in the background. Those pictures create such a beautiful contrast in texture and light. Trying to blur the background slightly really adds a punch.

At one point, I somehow wound up on a gravel road (thanks, Google). The bike was drifting on me around corners. I had to keep the speed up to keep moving. Finally, I emerged safely back on the pavement again. I found the Needles and caught a glimpse of Mount Rushmore and Crazy Horse.

I rode past a biker who had broken down. I had to drive a mile or so to turn around safely. I went back. He was blowing oil out of the reservoir. He had help on the way, so I offered him water, sat with him for a while, and talked.

I crossed Sheridan Lake at sunset. A walkway led down to the water's edge, so I went down the path to draw in the view. Giant boulders lined the edge of the lake, in contrast to the sloping mountains across from where I stood. At sunset, the view was breathtaking. I got back into town after dark, but it was well worth it.

~

The next morning, I broke camp and headed out to do laundry and get some chow. Uncle Louie's was closed, and I guessed they needed a break after serving thousands of bikers.

While doing a load of laundry, I found the post office and mailed off the busted Nikon, a helmet, and some clothes I wouldn't need. The problem with doing laundry was the clothes had to get packed first; then, I could load the bike. It slowed the process of packing the bike and getting back on the road. My next stop was in Wyoming, at Devils Tower.

Every state I had come through since Pennsylvania didn't have helmet laws. I wore one anyway, much of the time, but there wasn't much traffic, so I strapped it up behind me.

The smell of sage filled the air. I could see it growing everywhere alongside the road. I thought back to about 2006 when I attended a Native American recovery meeting. They burn sage in an abalone shell (called smudging), which they say dispels bad energy. Traditionally the heavy smoke is wafted with a large feather, and individuals cleanse themselves with the smoke as it washes over them. If available, an eagle feather is used (only Native Americans are permitted to possess an eagle feather for rituals such as this).

As I neared the Tower, its immense figure protruding up from the Prairie was stifling. The closer I got, the more surreal it became. The traffic was backed up, and waiting in line, in the heat, on a motorcycle was little fun, but at least the card I had purchased at Crow Reservoir campground for national parks afforded me free entry.

I proceeded to the parking area and walked along the path with many others to get closer.

I could see trees with colorful pieces of cloth hanging from the branches. Some were pouches that contained something sacred to their depositor. I read a nearby sign that explained that, for centuries, the Tower was visited by people from all over the world and that it's been considered a sacred place for thousands of years. These pieces of cloth are offerings. Some contain remains or personal items of someone dear. I was spellbound. Photographs should not be taken of these offerings; it just seems disrespectful.

I climbed up on a rock above the trees and pulled my keys from my pocket. Attached to my keychain was an aluminum cylinder containing some of my son Nick's ashes. I unscrewed the lid, removed the cap of the plastic insert, and began to sprinkle some of him before me. I thought of Nick and his older sibling Dave, watching the movie, Close Encounters of the Third Kind. I spoke a prayer of release. I sat quietly, reminiscing about their childhood, knowing I could have done better as a father but grateful that today I am sober. It all begins with that. It was very emotional for me.

As I left the park, there were a couple of places I stopped to get photos of the Tower, one with the bike in the foreground.

Once I was back on the road, traffic was pretty quiet. I was heading south toward Casper. The smell of sage still filled the air. I passed through several small towns. It was a hot one today.

I came across a train alongside the road just over an hour later. It was all engines. I was traveling at 60MPH for close to five minutes. Two sets of rails deep, I counted over 500 engines. I stopped and took a video, but it didn't capture what I saw.

I wound up along Wyodak Power Plant Road, near Donkey Creek. I stopped at the CBH CO-OP, a local eatery, and Truck Plaza for fuel and chow. There were a couple of bikes parked when I pulled in. One had its lights on, so when I walked inside to get some food, I spotted the two bikers and told them the lights were on.

I was maybe thirty or forty miles down the road and was intrigued by these funny-looking wood structures I saw along the road. They resembled bleachers, and they were on both sides of the road. It took a minute or so to figure out what they might be. I later found out my suspicion was correct, snow fences.

They are certainly different from the snow fences I recall working for the Salem County Bridge Dept. They were ⅜" slats of wood, 1½" wide, about 3' high, held together with maybe #12 wire. It came in a 50-75 feet long roll, propped up by steel posts along the road. The snow would drift up at the fence and not across the road. These were much more substantial.

Along Garner Lake Road, there were entrances to the ranches and oil wells every so often. I wanted a quick nap and pulled into one of them. There was virtually no traffic, and I guessed these didn't get much use. I assumed the position for a little bit of a snooze.

After 5 o'clock, I got ready to shove off again, and I saw those same two bikers pass me up. They waved as I pulled out behind them. I had no interest in catching up, though, so I watched them as they disappeared in the distance.

Here I was again, pretty much alone on a long stretch of highway, with nothing but the sound of my engine and peacefulness all around me as far as I could see, in every direction. The smell of sage filled the openness. I wondered if this was what cowboys of the old west had experienced, although at a much slower pace.

I stopped at another gas station, Midwest Sinclair in Edgerton. As I pulled up to the pump and shut the bike down, I looked at myself in the mirror. I was getting pretty weathered from the sun. I began fueling up when a beautiful woman emerged from the car next to me. She smiled and asked how I was.

As always, I responded, "Pretty good for an old fat guy." I thought possibly she was local, so I asked, "Do you know of a campground nearby?"

She replied, "I own a campground, Devils Tower KOA."

"Well," I continued, "I just left there this afternoon. I'm headed south to Casper."

I commented on how I love the empty roads, the scenery, and the smells. Florida is great but getting out of town and on the road is amazing. I explained that I'd love to get a ranch with ten or fifteen acres.

She stopped me. "Ten or fifteen acres is not a ranch. My husband and I own 7,000 acres. That's a Ranch."

I conceded, and she smiled.

While I was there, I booked an Airbnb in Casper.

It was a "Sheep Trailer" hosted by Steve. I explained that I'd be riding a fairly heavy motorcycle and asked if there would be an issue getting to him.

He replied, "No."

I was told to drive about two miles along a gravel road until I came to a gate, then turn. These bikes are not great on gravel roads. When I turned into the property, I realized I was in a pasture with uneven ground. I bounced up and down and side to side like a car in a 1940s cartoon.

Steve heard me and walked out to greet me. It was after ten.

I had eaten and was tired. The sheep trailer was reminiscent of a Conestoga wagon; it was about five feet wide by seven to eight feet long. The covered roof was canvas, I believe. The inside was a patchwork quilt. It was small but actually warm and quite cozy.

The bathroom was outside. It consisted of a Porta Potty (which was clean), and the shower was constructed of PVC pipe with a shower curtain. Hot water was instant from an LPG tankless heater. It was all so perfect.

Looking from this vantage point, the lights of Casper twinkled below. It was nothing less than amazing. Steve asked how I liked my coffee and promised to have it at first light, which he did.

After settling in, I got naked, walked outside to the open shower, and adjusted the water temperature. The night air was cool, and the hot water felt invigorating until it was time to turn it off. Then, the night air had its way with me. I was so cold I could hardly walk, gasping for air and staggering my way barefoot and naked, without my towel, the 50-75 feet or so to warmth. (Holy shit, was that stupid!) Once inside the sheep trailer, I was fine. Mistake #2 "Always take a towel."

I slept pretty well. Steve woke me early and gave me some suggestions for breakfast. As I made my way back down the rugged road, I came to a stop sign. Across the street were old wagon wheels buried halfway to mark the front of the property; there were dozens of them. I grabbed my phone and took a couple of pictures.

A patrolman pulled alongside me. He asked if I was ok. I guessed he was just sizing me up. I replied with a smile and said, "Yeah, just passing through."

He pulled away.

I found a recovery meeting at the 12-24 Club in Casper, a foundation that housed AA, NA, and ALANON meetings in the same building, each with its own rooms. There were small breakout rooms for Sponsor/Sponsee get-togethers, a full cafeteria that delivered food to you during the meeting, and a drug court in the basement. Dan showed me around. I had never in my sober years seen such a place.

After the meeting, I got on the road pretty quick and headed to Laramie. I was on my way to Colorado to see my old friend Todd.

We made a connection fifteen years ago in St. Pete. He landed probably the only snow-ski instructor job in the Great State of Florida at Bill Jackson's. Bill Jackson's had a carpet-covered ramp like a conveyor used for ski lessons. He also taught snowboarding and had done so in Colorado and, I believe, Utah. Todd moved back west seven or eight years ago. He's a real handsome, quiet guy. He could easily pass for Johnny Depp's brother.

Ours is a relationship such that we rarely speak to each other. We don't need to. We care about one another and feel the connection that goes beyond words, regardless of the miles between us. You know, I have a few friends with whom I share that connection.

Todd couldn't get away at that time and offered to house me in a hotel in Laramie. I rode around town, checking things out. I found "Bart's Flea Market" on the south side of town. What a great place. They had old horse-drawn buggies (different types), a 1963 VW microbus in great condition, Western boots, saddles, clothing, and housewares. I spent over an hour in that place. I really could've spent a fortune. Being on a Motorcycle saved me. Bart met me later at the front of the store, and we chatted for another half hour.

I returned to the hotel, where two other motorcycles were parked in the back. One had Arizona tags, and the other, I believe, was New Hampshire. The following morning, I began packing the bike. The two other gentlemen were packing theirs. They were brothers who were about my age. They lived in two corners of America and met in Tennessee.

They had been traveling together, all over the southwest, on their bikes. One was a BMW, the other a Honda. I thought it was great that two brothers explored the world together after spending most of their adult lives apart. Now reunited, as they've both retired, the priorities shifted. My thoughts went to my son David. With the loss of his brother Nick, he will never experience a trip with the brother he grew up with.

By early morning, I had made my way to Colorado. It was so strange that the topography changed so drastically. I stopped along the way and took a few photos, but I certainly would have taken many more if I had time. I stopped in Fort Collins for coffee at a 7/11 on the north side of town. Kids were walking to school as I sat on the curb drinking my coffee. They were ducking into the store and plugging up the restroom. Other customers seemed angry. It was a busy place, with plenty to watch.

Todd contacted me and explained he would not be able to make it today, so I got a room in Denver. I rode around to Boulder, checking out the area. I stopped at a gas station to get a bottle of water. They had a strange vending machine outside. The guy sat in a small booth behind bulletproof glass. I wasn't sure how it worked; maybe I would pay him, and he'd push a button to dispense the bottle of water or soda.

I approached the glass to ask about the cost. All I could smell was skunk bud coming from the booth. The kid was so stoned he couldn't keep his eyes open. He just sat and looked at me when I posed my question, so I asked again.

Through glassy eyes, he stuttered and stammered, "Umm, uh… I think it's like two, no, four. Uh, wait… I'm not really, um… Maybe like two dollars or something."

As he spoke, I slowly twisted my head from side to side, watching this stumble through the 4th grade. I just walked away thirsty and got two bottles at a nearby Walgreens. I'd already had enough of Denver, and I hadn't gotten there yet.

McDonald's was paying people eighteen to twenty dollars an hour. I seriously doubted they were getting their nickel's worth. I wanted to leave Colorado immediately. The traffic sucked. It was worse than Tampa. If I had to choose to live in Denver or Baltimore, I'd choose Baltimore.

I checked into the hotel and hit the pool. Some guy commented on the bike, which was fairly common; the Softail Slim draws quite a bit of attention. But he began to tell about how his bike was stolen by a guy he was gonna sell the bike to, but then he wound up in jail and blah, blah, blah. I half-listened to his tale. And none of it was his fault. And less and less made sense. I figured I'd just save him a seat next to me in a meeting.

The next morning, I started calling bike shops. I wanted a new front tire, and it was time for another oil change. Mark's Motorcycle Repair seemed like the place to go. Todd met me there. We loaded most of my gear up in his truck, and off we went.

Around Colorado

Todd picked me up at Mark's Motorcycle Repair in Englewood. We headed west in his truck on Route 285. It was very scenic. Riding shotgun allowed me to take lots of photos and some videos. I'd never seen the Rocky Mountains up close like this. We listened to some Grateful Dead as we tooled along the highway.

I had started a Facebook Group called "Roadtripgypsys" for another trip I had planned with my daughter Lorian years before. My daughter changed her mind about going, though. She had traveled back and forth to Tennessee that year with her mama and wasn't interested.

The plan was to set her up with a laptop or tablet and a website called Roadsideamerica.com. It lists tons of "B" attractions all over America. I would let her choose what we would experience and post photos and videos. It seemed like it would be a fun trip. The group has remained dormant until now. I invited lots of friends and family and began posting photos and uploading videos. I wrote stories and shared other parts of the trip in my downtime.

Todd and I grabbed a hotel in Frisco, a charming village. We got in late, had dinner, and returned to the hotel, where we could continue to talk. Todd had some catching up to do at work in the morning, so I had some time to kill and ventured out on foot for coffee and a little retail therapy.

We got on the road and made our way to Rifle, Colorado, to pick up leaf springs and three extra spare tires for the trailers. Some of the terrain getting to the remote cell towers could be rugged. Keeping the trucks and trailers in good working order was critical.

We hit a Walmart to get a couple of pullovers. When we drove to Glenwood Springs, I realized I'd lost my wallet. Todd suggested I call Walmart, which I did. They had the wallet, and the contents were intact.

It was here, in Rifle, we'd spend the next couple of days. We caught an AA meeting in Carbondale. Mt. Sopris came into view as we neared the town. It was the most majestic mountain I had ever seen. We found the facility and stepped from the truck. At the edge of the parking lot was a drop-off. Probably 500 feet or more below us was a beautiful skate park complex. The backdrop was Mt. Sopris. What an amazing view.

We stopped for pizza on the way back to Glenwood Springs. I had an allergic reaction to something. At first, I thought it was sunburn on the back of my head. My head itched and it proceeded around my neck, down my back, then over my whole body, even to my feet. I couldn't stop scratching. I tossed and turned all night. My bottom lip felt like a block of wood.

We drove to a pharmacy the next morning, where I grabbed some Benadryl that helped. We then retrieved my wallet and headed up to Craig, Colorado, with

Todd's crew and stayed one night there. Then, returned to Denver via Rt. 40.

The mountains were breathtaking. We stopped at Steamboat Springs and a couple of other little towns to find thrift shops. Todd often stopped at places for me to take photos of the beautiful landscapes. His truck is 4-wheel drive, so we did take a couple of dirt roads to find better shots in particular spots.

The mountain lakes reflected the deep-blue Colorado skies, surrounded by majestic mountains, all topped off with a sprinkling of beautiful white cumulus clouds. There were dirt roads in the distance that seemed to run forever up and over the mountains. Some of the mountains had ski slopes.

Byers Canyon winds along the Colorado River. This is a must-see. We found a couple of places to stop and absorb the sounds and sights of the river as it headed south through the Grand Canyon and onward to the Pacific Ocean. The rocky cliffs that surround the river in this area offer visual contrast to the smooth, sloping mountains in the distance.

As we climbed higher and higher on the road to Berthoud Pass, I could see that the mountaintops were bare of trees. Todd explained the oxygen is so thin that trees cannot survive here. Todd also informed me that avalanches had pushed down the toppled over trees. Many times, in the winter months, these roads are impassable. A road he had wanted to take a few days before was washed out by a mudslide.

We pulled into a parking area at the top of the pass, which is the "Continental Divide," at 11,300 feet above sea level. I jumped from the truck and rapidly walked to the overlook at the other end of the parking lot. I quickly slowed, then had to sit halfway there. There was not enough oxygen to support my old, fat ass. I pretended to be ok. I had far too much pride to admit I was that out of shape.

Too soon, the Rockies were behind us, and we were closing in on Denver again. I hated the traffic and wanted to turn back the hands of time, but I wasn't quite sure how far... two hours?... 100 years?

When my bike was ready, I said goodbye to my friend Todd. I hugged and thanked him for his treasured time and hospitality. I had arranged for an Airbnb in Denver. It was twenty bucks and a hostel, which is typically fine.

I rode north through Denver, past Mile High Stadium, grabbed a bite, and found my "home for tonight." The back gate was easy to find, and I opened it and walked into the back porch. There was a sofa, a TV, a chair, and a coffee table with a large bag of marijuana labeled "for free, help yourself."

With a furrowed brow, I looked up to see in front of me a hammock, surrounded on one side by rather large marijuana plants. Now I've been sober for over twenty-five years. I had no interest in any of this, but there I was in the middle of a place I would have loved to be when I was a teen.

I found the restroom inside, along with the owner. He noted that my accommodations were the hammock outside, which was fine. People came and went all evening. I made the hammock mine for the night.

I was wrestling with direction; I wasn't certain if I wanted to continue west or head home. Besides, I still wasn't feeling 100% after the allergic reaction. I considered heading back into Wyoming to see Yellowstone, then into the northwest along the coast. Or possibly back to Route 40 to find Route 50 through Nevada, "The Loneliest Road in America."

That would take me to Sacramento. My nephew Tim, Jeff's brother, lives near Lake Berryessa. I could hang with him and his three grown children, Pat, Frank, and Cassandra. From his place, I could head south along the Pacific Coast Highway to San Diego. I have a friend,

Nick, who lives there. Then I would catch Old Route 66 east, as far as it would take me, then I would cut over to the west side of the Appalachian Mountains, down through the Smokies. I would eventually hit Macon, Ga.

I figured I'd attend an early morning AA meeting and figure it out from there. Tonight, my mind was just cluttered with stuff. I've found that's never a good time to decide.

I woke up before daybreak, packed up, and went to get coffee. I caught a meeting and decided I was done. I needed to get closer to home. Katie had found a place to move to. I had spent enough cash and would need to tap into the HELOC had I continued. I didn't think that was prudent. At first, I set the navigation to "avoid highways," as always, but I switched it over after an hour or so.

This was the first time I was on a highway since Casper, and even then, I was only on that highway for ten or fifteen minutes.

From Denver, traveling east is pretty flat and uneventful. Rather than stop at the chain truck stops for food, I preferred pulling into small-town America and looking for a diner. Most are folded up, and they're harder and harder to find. At highway speeds, I put 450 miles behind me that day.

At a welcome station in Kansas, an agent informed me that pitching a tent on the grass at any rest area in Kansas was acceptable. My plan was made. As I continued east, I shifted myself around on the seat, for comfort, from time to time. At one point, I opened my legs wide and felt something out of place. I looked down, and the breather cover bolt had come out. The wind at 80 miles per hour was pushing the cover off. I reached down with my right hand, but the bolt was missing, and I had to fight with the cover, to keep it from blowing away. I hit it back in place and held it with my legs for twenty-five miles.

I came to a small town and started looking for a repair shop, but it was after 6, so I knew most places would be closed. I finally found an Auto Zone that was open. The missing bolt was a 1/4-20 Hex head bolt, ¾" long. I also needed a flat washer. I put it together, paid the fella, and fixed the bike.

Probably another hour down the road, I hit bad weather. I pulled into a rest area, parked the bike, and walked to a covered picnic bench. I got some rest there for an hour or so, using the rain gear as a pillow. The concrete picnic table wasn't very inviting, but it worked.

I got back on the road when it looked as though the weather was clearing, but it was only temporary. I got behind some trucks, and even though the road spray was something to deal with, I could follow the lights with some assurance of safety.

I stopped a few more times, resting as I could. Doing this, I drove off and on all night. At 3:30 am, after a stretch where I had been riding for almost an hour, I decided to get back off the highway and slow it down a bit. I covered a lot of ground on the interstate, but I needed to get back to Rural America.

Rural America

When I talk about Rural America, I mean not just back roads but small towns with just a few hundred or a couple of thousand people. I grew up in Southern New Jersey. It's a pretty area, and not much has changed in sixty years, but everything around it has. It's twenty minutes from the Philadelphia International Airport, two hours from New York City, one hour from Baltimore, and two hours from Washington, DC. It's right across the Delaware River from Wilmington, Delaware, and there is a twin-span bridge across the river just outside of town. But this area is somehow overlooked. A ten-minute ride from almost anywhere in South Jersey puts me in some beautiful farm country.

Florida, where I now live, is Paradise, but traffic is heavy and risky. Builders and investors are swallowing up the open land. Prices are skyrocketing, and lower-income people cannot afford to stay here. The part of America I wanted to see was all around me now. I just wanted to absorb its breadth.

I left the rest area at 3:30 a.m. and got back on I-70 eastbound, stopping at a Love's Travel Center in

Abilene, KS. I needed some coffee. They were brewing fresh, so I had to wait. The clerk offered me a complimentary coffee for my time—what a great way to start the day.

I made my way south from Abilene in the early morning light, allowing me to see the vast farmlands. Soon, the sun was coming up on my left. I rode past an old wooden windmill, but I just had to turn back to find the perfect place to take a picture with ole' Phoebe rising just behind it. The promise of a new day, another chance at a life that is unimaginable, was here.

I watched the sun get higher and higher in the early morning sky as I rode south. It seemed like someone should write a song about this moment in time.

I knew I would turn east and have the sun in my eyes at some point. I had sunglasses with me, but the glare would be difficult, so I planned that my morning would include a nap somewhere quiet. As I pulled into Eldorado, I saw a sign along the road that read "Wichita," and I began singing Glen Campbell's "Wichita Lineman." I can't help myself with that stuff.

Eldorado was a cool town. For some reason, it made me want to sing "Desperado" by the Eagles. I think maybe I hadn't had enough sleep.

A cop followed me around for a minute as I rode around town.

I found a little restaurant, had a bite to eat and was on my way in short order.

As I expected, the sun was in my eyes, so I looked for a spot to rest for an hour or so. I intended to wait until I got out of town a bit, and I found myself on Route 400, a smooth dual road with rolling hills and valleys and scenic farmland with little traffic. I think this was the beginning of the Ozarks.

A dirt road off to the side took me to a tranquil spot with enough shade to take a nap. After a bit of rest, I heard a pickup bouncing up the lane my way. The couple stopped and asked if I was ok. I thanked them and said I was better now, that "I needed a little rest."

I had driven most of the night, stopping now and then for short naps. It had been a long time since I pulled an all-nighter.

Back on the road, I continued for a few more hours. About 2:15 pm, I was getting sleepy again. My dogs have taught me a thing or two about life. When I'm tired, I nap. It works for my dogs; I figured it'll work for me. I follow this same routine at home, too.

I pulled off the road at the Robert E. Talbot Conservation Area, off of US Route 66. (I love old Route 66) I slept for about twenty minutes. As I got back on the road, I spotted a sign, "HANGAR KAFE," with an arrow. "How far can it be?" I asked myself.

So off I rode to find it. It was a couple of miles and a turn, a couple more miles and another turn, a couple more miles, and another turn until finally, I could see it ahead!

Ozarks Skydive Center and the Hangar Kafe are in a couple of airplane hangars, one of which is converted into a restaurant. I walked up, and a couple of women were sitting outside at the picnic table chatting. I felt they were possibly employees.

I entered the Kafe, and a waitress approached me. I asked if I could just look around since I had just eaten a short while back. Had I known I would be there, I would have waited. I bought a couple of bottles of water and took some photos.

As always, the bike created conversation. She asked me where I was headed and where I was from. We talked for a few moments, but I could see she was busy, so I asked, "Which one of the women out front would tell the best stories?"

She laughed and walked me out to introduce me to the others. We got distracted, and she showed me the antique vehicles sitting under the pole barn, a '59 Studebaker Lark (my old man had one) and two Studebaker pickups.

I sat with the ladies for a bit and talked with them. I believe it was all the same families that worked there. About then, a farmer in bib overalls strolled up. He was probably a few years my senior and the owner of the place. This was his farm, which had been in his family for generations.

He looked to be a pretty rugged old guy. He said he "wanted to learn to fly and do his own crop dusting, so he bought a plane and took some lessons to fly."

He loved flying and decided to open a skydiving center and a restaurant at the urging of others. He's still a farmer first and was on his way into town to catch the banks before closing. I thanked them all for the tour and headed back out.

I made it to Branson, Missouri, that afternoon. I booked another Airbnb. The instructions seemed clear once I arrived. "The top of the steps at the end of the hallway" was my room. There were no numbers on the doors, as in the description. I walked up the steps, turned left, walked to the end of the hallway, and opened the door.

To my surprise, the bed wasn't made. I thought it odd, so I reached out to Barb, the owner. She informed me I was at the wrong end of the hall.

This was where it all went a little south. I opened the door and saw the queen bed. A bottle of liquor, some makeup, and a corkscrew were on the dresser. I thought this was somewhat strange but proceeded to bring in my gear. I figured it was possibly the owner drank a little and maybe forgot they were there, or the previous border had left it.

I jumped in the shower in the hallway to wash three days of crud off me. I returned to the room and went through my things when I heard a woman's voice behind me asking, "What are you doing in our room?"

I assumed it was Barb, the owner, and exclaimed, "Oh, I thought you said this was my room—"

A guy with her interrupted me. He was a little angry.

About then, I realized they were customers as well. I apologized profusely and offered that there had to be an honest mistake somewhere. "Let's call Barb," I suggested.

I gathered my things and moved them back down the hall as they called the owner. Barb didn't realize she had rented the same room out to both of us. She had reached out to them earlier about upgrading to the king at the other end of the hall, where my things were. The fella had inquired about the upgrade first and had not checked his messages. He became angry at Barb, stating I had been in their room, and it appeared as though he was trying to leverage her. She was apologetic, but that wasn't satisfactory. I kept my nose out of it, but the guy was, in my estimation, a real asshat.

Barb came home shortly afterward to smooth things over. I made coffee for myself and sat in the kitchen. When she finished with him, she went into the kitchen and introduced herself. I invited her to sit with me and chat.

I began with an apology for creating an issue and asshat's behavior that followed, but she wasn't bothered by any of it. It seemed like she had a lot going on and made a simple mistake. We chatted some more, and it wasn't long before we found that she and I had another connection.

Barb had lost a child some years back. Her child died in a house fire. We talked about the hole that is left after losing a child. The dialog became very intimate and emotional. I was able to share some of the things that I've learned from the loss of Nick and the transformation we experienced. One of the things I shared about was when my son died. There were a few people whom I knew and thought cared but never called to acknowledge our loss.

At first, I didn't understand. I was hurt. Then I realized that it was very uncomfortable for them. Most folks don't know what to say. They understand the family is devastated and, possibly out of fear of saying something wrong, will avoid the whole thing. I got it!

I realized it was up to me to reach out to them through that pain. What I said was this, "I know that you love me. I know that you love Nick. I also understand it's difficult for both of us. You don't know what to say, and I don't know how to respond to what you don't know what to say."

I let them know that I'm grateful they're concerned about me, that's enough, and that I love them. That creates an atmosphere of healing this world is desperate for—simple understanding.

Barb shared a story with me. Her brother had called her from out of state. Recently a woman in his hometown lost a child in a house fire as Barb did years ago. This woman and her other children had escaped, but this one daughter was trapped in her room. The mother stayed on the phone with her daughter the entire time they tried to save her until the phone went dead. Barb called the woman, and they talked for some time. We realized that the experiences of the tragic loss of our children could be used to help other parents. With that knowledge, they have not died in vain.

That night my family got a little bigger.

I got a good night's sleep in that king-size bed and got up early. The soles were coming off my boots, and I didn't have time to fix them, so I threw them away and put on my sneaks. The ones I bought at a thrift shop when I was with Todd. As I grabbed my last bag, I put a $10.00 bill on the nightstand for Barb's son. He was the one that needed to put sheets on my bed, clean the hall shower I'd used the night before, and put up with that guy being nasty to his Mama.

He was downstairs getting ready for school. I heard the other tenant open his bedroom door as I headed downstairs. After I dropped the stuff out by my bike, I went back to the room and saw that the money was gone. That double-barreled asshole took it. I almost walked into his room to clean his clock, but I stopped myself. I didn't want to create an issue for Barb to untangle.

I walked back outside. A couple of minutes later, her son walked outside. I handed him a five-dollar bill (all I had left), but he refused it. He flat wouldn't take it. I pushed it into his pocket, and he pushed it back, stating he wasn't allowed to take it.

His Mama appeared and smiled at her son.

I wanted to tell her about "double-barreled Bob" but figured she had enough going on, and I guessed it'd catch up with him eventually. I said goodbye and rode off. It dawned on me. Letting go of it was that easy.

I'm asked from time to time why I still attend those AA meetings. I guess there are almost as many reasons as there are meetings. The most important reason is I have a problem digesting life sometimes. I tend to wallow in problems like quicksand. Usually, someone will throw me a rope in a meeting and help me out. Then again, every once in a while, I'm the one with the rope.

In the Christmas TV special, "Rudolph the Red-Nosed Reindeer," there's a part in the movie where Rudolph lands on the "Island of Misfit Toys." All the toys are deranged, mixed body parts on dolls, or put together wrong. That's kinda like the folks in recovery. We're all dented cans. There's no need to look up our noses or down our noses at anyone else. We're all the same. A level playing field. We're all trying just to be better people than we were yesterday and contribute to society positively.

As I left Branson, I looked for my next spot to eat and found a little store in Valley Springs, Arkansas. They had breakfast sandwiches available and a few tables next to the window. I ordered my food and walked to a cooler in the back to get a drink.

In the back, I saw what appeared to be local farmers who sat around tables. I think they were putting together a plan for the upcoming harvest. It reminded me of a place in Southern New Jersey. There was an old General Store in Harmersville, with raw wooden floors and a large front porch. Typically, these places sold groceries, livestock feed, and hardware.

I remember being there when I was working for Salem County in the winter months. There would be a bunch of old fellas sitting around telling stories. I thought those places were long gone from this world. I fell in love with this place at that instant. The rolling green hills in the Ozarks were quite peaceful and not yet screwed up by human "civilization."

I finished up my food and was off. It wasn't long before I discovered a park of sorts, "Grinders Ferry," at the Buffalo River. I turned around and drove back a half-mile and pulled down into what started as a paved entry. I found it was a riverbed of flat round rocks averaging about 3" in diameter at the base. Riding over them was easier than I presumed.

I rode probably a hundred yards, stopped the bike, and put down the kickstand. I checked it thoroughly for stability and walked over to a campsite. A fella and his boy were sitting in the "Buffalo River" in the water, relaxing as it trickled past them. This part of the riverbed is dry and can be driven on in summer. Where they were sitting was only a foot or so deep. In the springtime, I'm certain this can easily be flooded.

We were below the bridge, and I walked downstream along the creek. The man I spoke with said, "At one time, there was a rope swing. People would jump from it into the river. A Mountain Dew commercial had been filmed at this very location."

I've since looked it up on YouTube and found it probable. I thought this would be a great place to come back to and camp. Plus, it was free.

Riding up from the bottom, over the river rocks, was a little more troublesome than going down. I stopped atop the bridge and took several photos up and down the river. Down the road, a half-mile was an old barn. I stopped and took a few shots there, too, before heading out. Those places were where I missed the Nikon with the telephoto lens.

An hour or so down the road, I was on Route 124. I saw a sign that read, "Gravesville 2 miles." Below that, it said, "Quitman 10 miles."

Now there's something weird here. When a man quits, it could mean Gravesville for him. Am I the only one that thinks about stuff like this? Anyway, I was going to see what those towns were about. Gravesville, as I recall, turned out to be just a couple of houses. You might say it was, well, kinda dead.

I took a cutoff up the road a mile and turned left on Sequoyah Ranch Road. The Sequoyah Angus Ranch was large and what I believed to be the ranch house was beautiful. The fence surrounding this property was no joke. It looked to be metal tubing, and there was a lot of it. What started as a 600-acre Angus cattle ranch in 1994 is today over 3,000 acres. What an amazing drive it was through there. Beautiful farm country and an old, iron "camelback" bridge with a wooden deck across a creek. This made for a great photo op.

I followed this road until it dropped me at Lomax Rd. Soon enough, I was in sparkling downtown Quitman. I found a laundromat and did a load of wash. I had two pairs of jeans with me. The pair I was wearing would need to be laundered soon, and the other pair was ready. There were just a couple of people there.

I think laundromats are a great place to get the pulse of a town. When I first moved to Gulfport, Florida, I had an apartment on the beach. The building had its own laundry. However, I chose to use the laundromat that once stood on Beach Blvd., the main drag.

I met an older woman there. Her name was Loraine, and she would ride there on a three-wheel bicycle. It had been decorated for the July 4th parade with red, white, and blue streamers. They were faded by the rain and sun. Colorful tassels hung from the handle grips.

She slowly made her way through this sleepy little seaside art village. Loraine, with her white hair, was Americana at its best. I spoke with her several times while doing my laundry. I watched her get frustrated with the washer; it just wouldn't start. She had forgotten to put money in, and I was able to come to the rescue. When the popularity of this town exploded, the laundry was moved, then later closed forever. Some call it progress.

Here in Quitman, a woman and her mother were washing clothes. The daughter, I believe she was in her 50s, left for a few minutes and returned with ice cream cones. She purchased an extra one for the stranger. How thoughtful!

I thanked her. It was a hot summer day, and the ice cream sure was going to hit the spot. We talked earlier about life in this part of the world and other things like God. I avoided talking with folks about the pandemic. Not because of the polar arguments, but because I was just tired of hearing about it.

I'm not afraid to talk about God with folks, but I am careful. I guess maybe I see things a little differently than some people do. As a child and for most of my adult life, when something went haywire, people would say, "God is testing you."

But I started to think one time that if God has always been around and God had always known everything since before, He created all of this (that's what they say), then why the hell would God need to test me? I mean, didn't He always know what mistakes I would make? I think so. Maybe, just maybe, God is giving me the opportunity to test Him. In other words, if I'm upside down over something in my life and I know I cannot fix it, I can just ask God to handle it. Now, here's where it gets tricky. I can't have preconceived ideas about how things ought to turn out. A friend used to say, "Davy, everything is okay in the end. If it ain't okay, it ain't the end."

So, my job is to try to be nice to and help other people. God's job is to fix my life. That's pretty simple.

I wound up purchasing something I didn't need from the vending machine, dryer sheets, or something, and I offered them to the daughter, as my bags were full. I packed up and headed east when I passed what appeared to be a graveyard of Ford Mustangs. I turned once again. I couldn't miss this. I took a few photos.

There looked to be six rows of Mustangs, fifteen cars deep: convertibles, fastbacks, even a station wagon. (I'd completely forgotten they made Mustang station wagons). You name it; it was there. All '60s and '70s models, not much later than that.

That afternoon I crossed the Mississippi again. I turned onto an access road just after the bridge. I wanted to ride down to the waterfront along the Mississippi, but there was a casino and no way to approach the water, so I turned back.

I stopped at a store a little later, hoping for a sandwich. I walked in and looked around. The cashier was busy, and I could see it was just a convenience store with no prepared food. I made my way to the cashier when the customer left. I asked the attractive petite blonde if there was a sandwich shop nearby.

She pointed and said, "Down the road a bit," with a strong southern accent. Then she whispered, "He's an Indian, though," with a grimace.

I thanked her and turned with a straight face, but I found myself more than mildly amused at her prejudiced statement as I approached the door. I found an IGA that had burgers cooked, so that and soda did the trick, and I was on my way again.

It became dark during the past two hours of riding, and the weather turned. It rained a little. Traffic on the road was heavy. I was ready to stop at sunset but continued until I finally pulled into a gas station in Hamilton, Alabama. I tried to find an Airbnb, but the only thing I could find was a Motel 6.

It was after 10 pm. I had stayed in many a Motel 6 over the years. The name was derived from the fact the rooms were six bucks when it started. For most of the ones I'd experienced, I thought that even if they were still six bucks, it would be a questionable price. But this particular Motel 6 was really clean, everything worked, and the bed wasn't screwed flat. I got squared away and rode off to get some chow.

The only thing I found open was Domino's pizza. They were closing, but I pleaded with the girl to feed me, and she did. The problem was, I was on a motorcycle, and I wanted to go back to my room to eat, not sit on the sidewalk, so I would have to get clever. I leveled the Ram phone mount, tightened it up, laid the small pie on top, and used a small bungee cord in the saddlebag to secure it. It worked! I made it to the room, and so did the pizza.

The following morning, I was ready to get back on the road. I needed coffee. Someone at the motel told me Hardee's coffee was the way to go. I figured, "Okay, I'll try anything once, if I'm not sure, maybe twice."

Let's just say that between the half-hour wait and the coffee-flavored hot water they sold me; it was pretty unlikely that I'd return.

Much of the roadway from the Mississippi to here was beautiful. I did access the highway for a short time the night before coming into Hamilton. The city itself seemed very laid back. Heading southeast on 278 turned out to be one of the more scenic roads I'd travel. Several pastures with beautiful trees looked like a great place for family picnics.

I wasn't far out of town when I spotted a long red dirt road that seemed to disappear over the hill. I stopped and photographed it. I wanted to take that road just to see where it led, but the gravel looked much too soft for this bike. A mile or so beyond that was a paved road that ran the same direction. I figured I'd do better on this road, Marion County Rt. 57. I turned right, and off I went.

At the crest, the view was spectacular, even though I could see that much of the hills were covered by Kudzu. The trees are overrun with this invasive species. I decided to follow this road until the end. It was very scenic, and I don't think I passed a single car.

I landed back on 278 and had seen signs for the Natural Iron Bridge. This is the largest natural bridge east of the Rockies, so I checked it out. As I turned into the driveway, a large metal sign crossed it above the gate, "Natural Bridge."

I pulled into the parking area and entered the privately owned facility. The entry fee was a mere three dollars. I paid and followed another couple out toward the bridge. I helped them get some photos, and they took a couple of pictures of me. The whole place took about an hour or so to get through. I felt I had plenty of time. It was about a 6-1/2-hour drive and 320 miles to Macon, from Hamilton. The weather was perfect, not a cloud in the sky. I figured I'd take my time today and sightsee.

As I walked back toward the entrance, I saw a sign, "Indian Face." I explored that area and found a spot where people had balanced stones, an ancient meditation practice. I found several flat stones and constructed my own small "stack."

I pulled my keys from my pocket again and opened the aluminum capsule that housed my son's ashes. I sprinkled just a minute amount over the stack, then offered a prayer and left.

As I exited the park, I realized the overhead metal sign that said: "Natural Bridge" was, in fact, backward, which meant if I took a selfie underneath, it would appear correctly, which was the case.

I wonder if other people ever asked themselves, "Why does my selfie camera on the phone make everything appear backward?"

I don't guess most people think about things like that, but I do. It's just a guess, but most people, when photographed, don't like the picture. *It doesn't look like me*, they think.

Well, there's a reason we think like that. The only time we see ourselves is in a mirror. We see ourselves backward. That's what we're accustomed to seeing. A front-facing photo looks different. So the "selfie" imaging on cell phones "flip" the exposure to be more acceptable to the person taking the selfie. Does that make sense?

I continued along 278. The smell of honeysuckle filled the warm summer air. It was intoxicating. It was all I could smell as the miles rolled past unless it was interrupted by someone mowing grass.

I stopped in Cullman, Alabama, at Rumors Deli. The inside of the place was great. It's an old brick warehouse converted into a restaurant. It would've been a great place. They were pretty busy for a Saturday afternoon, but my salad was small and uneventful. One small tomato. It was like eight bucks. Not impressed, I rode off hungry.

I passed a place called The Haunted Chicken House in Cleburne, AL. I had no idea what this place was until I looked it up on WWW but driving by it got my attention. I thought it was a restaurant. Out front was several old Ambulances, hearses, and limousines, some with their noses stuck in the ground and some piled high—another great photo opp. I spun around and went back. I think it's some kind of haunted attraction in rural Alabama.

As I crossed the mountains, the weather changed abruptly. It began to rain, so I stopped and put on the rain gear. I pulled into an Exxon station at WestPoint, Georgia, at about 6:45. I needed coffee and a snack. I knew I still had a couple of hours, maybe three, to travel.

Once it began to get dark, the rain made it difficult to see. My glasses had spots of water on them. It was like trying to look through bubble wrap. I bought Rain-X for the windshield a few days before and used it a few times, but it didn't help as much as I would've liked. I had to keep my speed up high enough for the raindrops to blow off. But that didn't help my glasses and wiping them was useless.

I had already booked an Airbnb in Warner Robins, GA., just south of Macon. It was dark and continuing at night in the rain, was dangerous, so I reached out to beg off the rental, but the owner didn't respond. I wanted to find something closer. I stopped at another gas station in a town called Waverly Hall. I asked about a motel, and the young fella told me it was thirty miles in the wrong direction.

I needed a bathroom by now. Coffee had that effect on my bladder, but his bathroom was closed. He directed me to the Dollar General in the shopping center next door.

As I rode through the parking lot, I spotted an old car wash. It was abandoned and dark. It looked like it had been closed for months, if not years. I figured I could at least pull in to get out of the rain for a bit. There was brush growing in front of the last bay. It looked like a great spot to whizz, and I didn't think I'd make it to the Dollar General anyway.

As I pulled in, I could see the slope of the floor was pretty drastic. The drain in the center was about 2 ft x 3 ft. When the front wheel of the bike cleared the hump, my headlight pointed down, and I could now see that the grate was missing. I was headed right for that big hole.

I swerved at the last second and just missed plunging my front end into a pit over a foot deep. That would have ended the trip. I thought I was gonna have a heart attack. By now, I had to pee really, really bad.

As I was about to put the kickstand down, my phone rang. So now, I was trying to get off the bike, not accidentally pee, and get the phone out of the holder to catch the call. It was a friend, Mark, who I hadn't talked to in decades –perhaps four decades.

I was just about to piss myself. I was wearing a rain suit with a Velcro fly and a zipper, and the zipper on my jeans and the fly on my boxers. I fumbled around one-handed while listening to Mark. My jeans were soaked, and I was cold, making "things" much more difficult. I started to pee, and I wasn't sure if I "cleared the holster." I figured, "Well, at least it will be warm."

Mark had been following my trip on Facebook, along with a few others. We were neighbors many years ago. I was pretty humbled that he was so appreciative that I was sharing this journey with family and friends, many of whom had been stuck at home since Covid. He and a couple of other friends inspired this writing. We spent about forty-five minutes catching up.

By the time we ended the call, the rain had stopped. I got back on the bike and headed out. Ten minutes down the road, the rain started again, but it also got foggy this time.

The speed limit was 55 or 60. There was no shoulder to pull off safely, and by the time I saw a crossroad, I'd passed it already. There was no way I'd turn around.

The spots of water on my glasses were like tiny magnifying glasses. I could see the reflectors in the middle of the road until a car came the other way. Then I could see nothing. When I'd pass a yellow reflective road sign warning of an upcoming corner, it would blind me from seeing almost everything else. I tried wiping my glasses, but that smeared them and made it worse. I knew I couldn't slow down. If a car were to come around a corner from behind at the speed limit, I'd get whacked, and there were lots of corners.

Of course, as if that wasn't enough to be concerned with, my imagination kicked in. I could imagine a deer bolting out in front of me, killing both of us. If there were potholes or other road hazards, I couldn't see them. I wasn't as worried about myself as I was about the bike. I loved my bike. I didn't want it to crash off a mountain. I prayed, "Dear God, if I get to another town, I'll sleep on the sidewalk."

I haven't told you that I had been diagnosed with epiretinal membrane. That's something I had never heard of before. My eye doctor explained that I have wrinkles in the back of my eyes, which distort my vision. Glasses help with the focus, but what I see is distorted or kind of smeared; the left eye is at least twice as bad as the right eye. When I look at a vertical straight line, it is wiggly (both eyes are opposite). A horizontal line is also wiggly with the left eye only. If I look at a basketball, it's the shape of a football. It's common in older folks like myself. It's one of the motivating factors for taking this trip in the first place. I'm not certain how long I'll be able to drive safely. Once I cannot, I will reassess things.

I forged ahead, gripping the handlebars tight, my butt cheeks squeezing the seat. I was just trying to calm myself, but every turn seemed treacherous. "What if a car came around the corner in the wrong lane?"

The questions plagued me.

Eventually, after what seemed like hours, I pulled into the next town and found another gas station with an overhang. This station was in a seedy part of town. I was a little nervous, to say the least. I approached the clerk inside and inquired whether there was a motel nearby, but the answer was the same as the last place. I wasn't ready to travel forty minutes in the wrong direction.

I stepped outside and sat on the curb in front of my bike and attempted to text Salah, the host of the Airbnb in Warner Robins, to no avail. As I sat there, looking at my blank phone, trying to figure out what to do next, I could see a tall black fella over my left shoulder staring at me. He reminded me of Morgan Freeman, but he looked a little meaner (maybe quite a bit meaner). It seemed to me he wasn't happy about this white stranger hanging around his corner. I looked around and felt very uncomfortable.

Now here I was in a place I had prayed for. Safe from the backroads of hell (I'm sure they're beautiful on a sunny day), but I feel threatened by something else.

I tried one more call to the Airbnb, then lowered my head and said a quick prayer. It went something like this, "Ok, I know I said if I got here, I'd stay, but I'm going to have to trust You with a few more miles. If I get whacked, I get whacked doing something I love. My life is in Your Hands."

I mounted the bike and rode off.

I followed behind a car, as I had done earlier. I felt safer, as I could trust their ability to see ahead and could follow the taillights easily. Unfortunately, as before, the car would turn off, and I would have to proceed alone. The rain continued, but the fog had stopped before I arrived in Talbotton, GA. About ten minutes later, the rain slowed to a stop, and I began to see stars as the night sky cleared. I dried my glasses once more and continued through a couple of other small towns, including Butler.

I arrived at my destination at about 11:00 pm. The host was fast asleep on the sofa as I walked through the door, which explained why he didn't respond to my messages. He was from Madagascar, working here as an Uber driver. We chatted for a bit before he left. He explained he had a shift. He drives when it gets busy and sleeps in between. He had told me earlier he didn't want me to rent a room because the water line had broken that morning, and it would be Monday before it was fixed. I said, "I don't care. I just want a place to crash."

He offered to give me two nights for the price of one, so tonight, I'd make do without a shower. I had stopped at a restroom on the way and figured his bushes might need to be watered before daylight.

The next morning, I woke up and headed out for coffee and breakfast. I plugged in the address for the H&H Soul Food restaurant in Macon. I wanted to visit the Big House, where the Allman Brothers had lived. They would walk from there to the H&H for breakfast. I found this bit of interesting history from Wikipedia...

The restaurant was started in 1959 by Mama Hill in another location and later settled into its current home.

"Struggling musicians from The Allman Brothers Band put together enough money to buy two meals for the band to share. Mama Louise felt sorry for the hungry musicians and brought them their meals and told them to pay her when they had the money. This was the beginning of their friendship; they always knew they could count on Mama Louise when times were hard. After the band became famous, they invited Mama Louise on tour with them in 1972 to California to fix their meals. However, she never cooked a single thing." (Wiki)

The walls were covered with AB memorabilia, autographed photos, and awards, and their music played continuously. It was a very busy place early Sunday morning, but then again, most restaurants are.

After breakfast, I headed to Rose Hill Cemetery, where the Allmans are laid to rest. I rode around the cemetery, thinking I could find the tombs on my own, but I could not. I rode back to the entrance after fifteen minutes or so and looked at the map.

I could download a map for a few bucks, but I knew they were in Carnation Ridge. I returned to find it immediately. I parked the bike in front of the large plot at the end of the dirt road. I walked up to see the finished product.

I was there with Katie in December of 2018. This memorial was under construction then. When we arrived, a fella was there laying bricks. I started talking before I got to him. He turned and nodded. I asked what he was doing, and he replied that he had been employed to build this memorial. I explained that we were there to pay respects to the Allman Brothers. I had seen them when Duane was still alive, in May of 1971. He told me that he had come up with Greg, which I assumed meant they went to school together. I told him that I was a tile guy, and we traded a few stories. Then he turned to the pallet of bricks as he said, "These were special made for this project."

He picked through them, found just what he wanted, and handed it to me as a gift. I offered him some cash, and he said, "Oh no! They pay me very well to do this work."

I asked if he would autograph it, and he was a little embarrassed but agreed. As we left, I looked at his name: Roscoe Ross. His family had been in the bricklaying industry for over 125 years. He was the "go-to" guy for the Macon area for all the historical renovations. I was talking with an icon in the brick industry.

Now, I stood in front of his finished work. I took a couple of pics of the Harley with the wall and steps in the background. I opened the saddlebags and took out the bag of sage I had collected out west. I burned a small bit of it and took photos and a video of the memorial. Then, I headed out to the site where Duane Allman wrecked his motorcycle on October 29th, 1971. I took photos of my bike there, too. From that point, I went to the Big House Museum. I picked up a new tee shirt and headed back to Warner Robins. I caught a meeting at the Alkanon Club that evening and again the next morning.

The next day, I had planned on stopping in Jacksonville, Florida, for the evening. I took off and made it to the Douglas, GA, Covered Wagon Country Buffet for lunch, then headed out. From there, I decided to find Rickerson Road. There looked to be one, thirty miles back, near Snipesville. I passed tobacco farms and cotton fields along the way. I was excited to see a road with my family name, so I didn't mind driving an hour and a half out of my way.

I came upon a sign that read Ricketson Rd. I didn't even stop but just headed back a different way. I wound up on another gravel road. I saw a couple of beautiful old barns along the way, which made for great photo ops. I even stopped and grabbed some tobacco to put in with the Sage.

This part of Georgia is very scenic. Northern Georgia has beautiful mountains and hills and rolling countryside. A bit further south, it gets pretty flat. I made it to Folkston, GA, by 4 pm and made a reservation at an Airbnb in Jacksonville. I got there just before dark.

I settled in, then hit a WaWa for dinner. They have five-star gas station food. I love their cheesesteaks, and in the fall, they have a Turkey Gobbler, a sandwich that is nothing less than amazing. Thick slices of real turkey, on a soft hoagie roll, slathered in gravy. You can choose to add stuffing, cranberry sauce, cheese, and much more.

This will more than satisfy any hankering one might have for a traditional Thanksgiving meal.

I got up about 4:30 the next morning and hit Wawa for coffee and a soft pretzel for breakfast. I wanted to go to the A1A and head south, but instead, I headed in the wrong direction for almost an hour and took Rt. 200 over toward the beach. I finally caught A1A in Fernandina Beach and headed south. From there, I took the Mayport Ferry and continued along A1A, once south of Jacksonville. This road is gorgeous, with the Atlantic Ocean on the left and pull-offs with beach accesses on the right.

It wasn't long before I pulled into St. Augustine. The college and the architecture of so many buildings there are fabulous. The narrow cobblestone streets are lined with shops of all sorts. I took some photos and tried

Facebook live. The videos I took underway were bouncy and unattractive. A GoPro would've worked nicely.

I had to get off the A1A to go through St. Augustine, then return east to resume the ride along A1A. There was no bridge at the inlet to connect Vilano Beach and Anastasia State Park. This whole area was just stunning with natural beauty. But leaving the beaches provided the opportunity to see the lighthouse and many other attractions.

Katie and I once toured The Florida School for the Deaf and the Blind. Children travel from all over this expansive state to attend one of the best schools in the world. It's such a wonderful experience to teach here that attrition is the only way to get hired. Like those from Key West (450 miles) or Pensacola (400 miles), some children fly into the boarding school Monday. Friday, they fly home for the weekend. The rest are bussed. Everything is designed to teach these young people how to excel with their lifestyle.

A1A is one of my favorite roads to travel. It was almost like I traveled this road in another lifetime. It just seemed so familiar. There were parking areas along the right to spend time at the beach. The parking fee was three dollars, and there were Porta Potties. A crossover with lights was there for safely crossing the road. Most of the parking areas were unoccupied, and I pulled into one.

I had a bathing suit, so I got naked in the parking lot and put it on. If someone had seen this old man naked, they'd have gone home and washed their eyes out with bleach.

Over to the beach, I went. I took a black and orange Harley Davidson bedroll that my son David had bought me for Father's Day. He had given it to me early, as Father's Day was the day after I left. I used it every time I camped. It would be perfect for the beach.

Once I got across the road and over the dunes, as far as one could see, there was no one to the south, and looking north, there was one woman a half-mile up the beach, walking away from me. As if the smell of the Atlantic air, the pounding surf with the gulls squawking, wasn't enough, the warmth of the late summer sun in the morning warmed my face as I lay on the beach alone. I thought about the miles behind me, the friends and family I visited, the places I had traveled to, and the folks I met. I'm sure some were for the last time.

I thought about what would lie ahead. A vacant home? Would I sell? Would I refi and fix a few things? Possibly make it into an Airbnb. I knew that I would begin to worry when I got to this spot. I get restless. I try to remember to reel myself back into the present. Things might not feel right; they might look like the world was upside down, but I now have all that I need.

I stayed for a half-hour or so, then headed to Daytona. I rode through the main street, then followed the GPS to my next destination. An old buddy, Phil, lives in Port Orange, so I stopped in to stay the night. He had a project I was more than willing to do, putting together a few sets of shelving for his office. We broke for dinner and went to one of my favorites in Daytona, "Steve's Famous Diner." The bread they served with the meal reminded me of a place where I grew up.

Priolios was a small Italian bakery with a brick oven. They made bread and dinner rolls, and one night a week, they'd make pizza. My dad would take me with him to get a loaf of bread anytime we had spaghetti (usually on Sunday). They'd give the old man a beer and me a pocketbook roll... they were usually still warm with a slightly hard crust.

Phil lives in the nicest mobile home park I've ever seen. There were beautiful, big lots for each home, old oak trees with the Spanish moss hanging from the limbs, and the lawns were all manicured and trimmed with tropical shrubbery. It was really hard to imagine those were mobile homes.

I got a good night's sleep and headed out early for the last leg of the trip. I was on International Speedway Blvd. when I spotted a woman broken down on the other side of the road. I spun around and went back to assist, but she informed me she had called her father-in-law, and he was on the way. I putzed around to see what the issue was, but I could not fix it.

It didn't seem like I would be much help, and I left just before her help arrived. It looked like it was going to rain, but I pushed ahead. I stopped for fuel at a Circle K in Seminole Springs, and while in the station, it began to rain. I put on the slicker. It was just a light rain at first, but as I headed west, it got heavier.

I went through Tavares and Groveland. As I neared Tampa, I needed fuel and a restroom. The restroom was the priority. The one station I stopped at had no restroom open. I'd always wondered where the hell the employees go to the bathroom. This was a question that had perplexed me for decades. Do they keep a bucket in the back? No, but I think I figured it out. They peed behind the dumpster out back. I won't tell ya how I figured that out.

I was on Harney Road, and now it was raining heavily. I merged onto I-4, and the rain was steady. My glasses fogged, and I had to look over their tops.

Traffic is always heavy at "malfunction junction" where I-4 and 275 intersected, so I stayed back to give myself room. Cars and trucks would pull in front of me, and I'd just slow down. I was already soaked to the bone. Both feet were soggy.

Once over the Howard Franklin Bridge, I pulled off on Gandy Blvd. I stopped at the WaWa there and bought a hoagie. There were a couple out front. They seemed to be tweakers to me. She was way too talkative, so I ate fast and jumped back on the bike. It was still pouring, and the closer I got to Gulfport, the harder the rain got. It took exactly five drenching hours to get home.

A total of 9,021 miles in seventy-three days, during which I spent approximately $4,000, including tires and oil changes. I got home safe. My wife and I were divorced on October 27th. I'm currently living with my two dogs, Jasper and Lucy.

I worried that I would lose Lucy while I was on the road. She's fourteen and still pretty spry, but she's moving slower each day. But upon my return, she was fine.

It's quiet here now. I love our home. I'm at the place in my life where I'm ok to be alone, and most of the time, I have no interest in leaving. I love when people come to visit. I love it when they leave.

I have no idea which way I'm headed. Everything is up in the air. I went to the eye doctor the other day, and she told me she thought my left eye might be healing, although it sure doesn't look like it from here. "We'll watch it," she said.

If this book sells, I might just take another trip next year. I want to see the Pacific Coast Highway and cut across Rt. 66. I'll be looking for places to stay and people to meet. There's a good chance my door will swing both ways. Winters here in Florida aren't all that bad, so if you have ideas of places I oughta check out, I'm anxious to hear about them. Send me an email at drickerson55@gmail.com

If you've lost someone you love to addiction or alcoholism, please visit the website: https://pathoftears.org

Epilogue

I'm not sure what I'm supposed to write here, but there are a couple of things I want to talk about, so here we go.

I have purposefully avoided chatter about "The Pandemic." Most of us have heard enough about it and need a break. Embarking on this journey in the midst of it made it difficult to eat, shop and try to be normal. In many places, dining rooms were closed, and take-out was all that was available. It's difficult getting comfortable on a bike with food.

But the hardest part for me was watching all of you. "Jab or No Jab?" The fighting between us. So many of my friends and family were under lockdown, unable or afraid to see people they love, and unable to hug each other, which is something I feel we're desperate for. We are so afraid of dying or losing someone close. But are we really living? My mom used to say, "No one gets out of this alive." At some point, we all cross that bridge.

I started thinking about what if, by chance, the human race would go the way of the dinosaur and become extinct. That might not be such a terrible thing. I mean, we're all gonna die anyway, right? Maybe

Mother Earth would be a better place without humans. No other mammal has trashed this beautiful blue planet more than we have. I sometimes wonder why she's not gotten rid of us already. We're devouring natural resources at an exponential rate for the almighty buck. Chasing happiness, we will never catch it until we stop.

The indigenous people in America have it right. They revere Mother Earth and their elders. They understand that everything is connected. We came here and bludgeoned them with our religion and way of life when we could have come here as students, learning how to live in harmony. I think we have moved so far from what matters. Could we, together, turn things around? I have no idea. I believe it's worth a try.

I refuse to live in fear of dying. If I have to live in fear, I prefer to fear that I will not live my life to its fullest. We're only here once. Time and health fade faster than anyone cares to admit. This trip was the beginning of something new. I have no idea what, but every day will be a surprise from this point forward. Care to join me?

Acknowledgment

I have so many people to thank for their help with this memoir. Janine Houser and Marsha Kaler both stepped up to help me edit this at the beginning of this endeavor. Their support, friendship, and encouragement have been so special. Steve Green for spending untold hours reading and rereading, editing, and offering his gentle guidance to make this what it is. Leila Kirkconnell, just when I thought it was ready, she stepped in and stepped up. She's responsible for many corrections and the cover. She offered her wisdom and expertise. Deb Sallee for giving us another set of eyes on this work.

I am truly indebted to these people for making this book a reality.

Mr. Gaffin, my English teacher. Even though I wasn't paying attention in class, he taught us something much more valuable than language; Ed taught us how to think outside the box and question authority... beginning with my own.

And finally, all my friends and family who are so much a part of my life and this incredible journey.

Made in United States
Orlando, FL
23 January 2023

28985053R00113